Evangelical Lutheran Synod and Ministerium of SC

Minutes of the Evangelical Lutheran Synod and Ministerium of South Carolina

and Adjacent States, Convened at Beth Eden Church, Newberry District, S.C., on the Fourteenth of October, 1864, and at St. Matthew's Church, Orangeburg, October Twelfth, 1865

Evangelical Lutheran Synod and Ministerium of SC

Minutes of the Evangelical Lutheran Synod and Ministerium of South Carolina *and Adjacent States, Convened at Beth Eden Church, Newberry District, S.C., on the Fourteenth of October, 1864, and at St. Matthew's Church, Orangeburg, October Twelfth, 1865*

ISBN/EAN: 9783337844806

Printed in Europe, USA, Canada, Australia, Japan

Cover: Foto ©Lupo / pixelio.de

More available books at **www.hansebooks.com**

MINUTES

OF THE

EVANGELICAL LUTHERAN

SYNOD AND MINISTERIUM

OF

SOUTH CAROLINA AND ADJACENT STATES,

CONVENED AT

BETH EDEN CHURCH, NEWBERRY DISTRICT, S. C.,

ON THE FOURTEENTH OF OCTOBER, 1864,

AND AT

ST. MATHEW'S CHURCH, ORANGEBURG,

OCTOBER TWELFTH, 1865.

The Minutes of the Synodical Missionary Society,

AND OF THE

Society for the Relief of Disabled Ministers, etc.

NEWBERRY:
PRINTED AT THE "HERALD" OFFICE.
1865.

Ordained Ministers Absent.

1. Rev. A. Angerer..Walhalla, S. C.
2. " B. F. Berry..................................Cowpen Branch, "
3. " C. H. Bernheim,..Ocala, Fla.
4. " E. Dufford..................................In Confederate service.
5. " F. Hickerson................................ " "
6. " W. A. Houck*...............................Orangeburg, S. C.
7. " A. W. Lindler*...............................Germanville, "
8. " J. P. Margart*...Eufaula, Ala.
9. " J. Moser*....................................Hope Station, S. C.
10. " L. Muller...Walhalla, "
11. " B. Kreps.....................................Edisto Mills, "
12. " M. Rauch*.....................................Germanville, "
13. " F. Wilken.......................................Wartburg, Tenn.
14. " J. H. W. Wertz*...............................Frog Level, S. C.

*Excused.

Licentiates Absent.

1. Rev. S. Baily.......................................Bufords Bridge, S. C.

Members ex-officio.

Mr. W. W. Houseal, *Treasurer of Synod.*
Mr. J. F. Schirmer, *Treasurer of Seminary.*
Maj. J. P. Kinard, *Treasurer of Widow's Fund.*

The lay delegates next presented their certificates, and were received as members of Synod:

Lay Delegates.

F. A. Brame....................	from	Rev. C. F. Bansemer's	charge.
A. G. Dickert....................	"	" T. S. Boinest's	"
P. E. Wise....................	"	" S. Bouknight's	"
J. H. Graman....................	"	" W. S. Bowman's	"
R. H. Zimmerman....................	"	" P. Derrick's	"
H. C. Franck....................	"	" A. R. Rude's	"
H. W. Rikard....................	"	" J. M. Schreckhise's	"
J. Setzler....................	"	" A. D. L. Moser's	"
Adam King....................	"	" B. F. Berry's	"
Dr. G. Muller....................	"	Sandy Run	"
J. G. Houseal....................	"	Rev. J. H. Bailey's	"
W. W. Houseal....................	"	" Prof. Smeltzer's	"

JACOB BARRE.................	from Rev.	E. Caughman's charge,
EDWIN KING.	" "	D. Sheely's "
D. NUNNAMAKER..............	" "	W. Berly's "
J. W. DREHER................	" "	D. M. Blackwelder's "
J. S. DERRICK................	" "	A. W. Lindler's "
J. F. SCHIRMER..............	" "	Dr. Bachman's "

Rev. G. D. Bernheim, of the Synod of North Carolina, was present, and invited to a seat as an advisory member.

Rev. W. Berly was excused for not attending the meeting of the General Synod, and Revs. E. Caughman and J. N. Derrick, delegate, and alternate elect to the Synod of North Carolina, presented their excuses for not attending, which being satisfactory they were excused.

The delegate to the Synod of Georgia read the following report, which was received and adopted, and expenses ordered to be paid.

REPORT OF THE DELEGATE TO THE SYNOD OF GEORGIA.

Your delegate appointed at your last meeting to attend the convention of the Synod of Georgia, met with that body at St. John's Church, in Spalding county, in July last, and met from the members of that body a most cordial reception. Your delegate though in a strange land felt that he was not a stranger there, as he stood surrounded by those who went out from our own Synod, and were licensed and ordained at our own altars. He took occasion to assure the Synod of the deep interest which we feel in their welfare, and our ardent desires and prayers for their prosperity, and was assured in return by the presiding officer of that body that our kindly feelings were sincerely appreciated and warmly reciprocated, while he also expressed the ardent desire that these friendly relations should be cherished and cultivated.

These brethren have a large and interesting field of usefulness before them, and since the valuable accession to their number of two more of our cherished and esteemed brethren, they have been inspired with renewed vigor for the cultivation and improvement of their large field.

We deeply sympathise with these brethren in the sad afflictions which they have been called to experience, in consequence of the polluting tread upon so much of their soil by the vandal foe, as has forced at least one of their number to flee from his home and from his people.

They appointed Rev. J. Hawkins, their delegate, to the present meeting of our Synod, whom we are pleased to see among us, and whom they charged with the duty of requesting this body to establish a boundary line between the two Synods, and of suggesting the Savannah river as that boundary.

My expenses amounted to fifty dollars.

T. S. BOINEST, *Delegate to Georgia Synod.*

Rev. W. Berly read the President's annual report. Received, and ordered to be referred to a committee.

PRESIDENT'S REPORT.

Dearly beloved Brethren:

In the good Providence of God, the lives of all the clerical members, composing this ecclesiastical body, have been spared during another Synodical year, and we are permitted to meet together in our annual Convention, and to greet each other once more in the land of the living. The cruel and sanguinary war which has raged for nearly four long years, is still carried forward with unabated fury. Many of the best and most efficient members of our Churches, have been sacrificed upon the altar of their country's liberty, and almost every house in this Southern land has become a house of mourning. Some sad reverses have recently befallen our arms. The outposts of Mobile have fallen, and the Gate City of Georgia has been evacuated by our forces, and occupied by the enemy. But still we have reason to thank our Heavenly Father, that our country has not yet been entirely overrun, and that much of our lost territory, has, during the past year, been regained. Our harvests in some sections have been light, but in others, we have been blessed with great abundance. Amidst all our disasters, and discouragements, therefore, let us confide in Him, who has promised to hear the right, and to succour the afflicted and oppressed. But allow me to turn away from these scenes of sadness and of sorrow, and give you an account of my official acts during the past Synodical year.

I. OFFICIAL.

1. Soon after the adjournment of Synod at its last regular meeting, I sent certificates of honorable dismissal from this body, to Revs. J. Hawkins and J. Austin, who have since connected themselves with the Synod of South Western Georgia. These brethren express their deep regret in parting from us, but felt it their duty to pursue the course they have hoping thereby to add efficiency to the new organization, and give encouragement to their brethren, who had first undertaken the enterprise. Your presiding officer assured them that the feeling of sympathy expressed, was reciprocated by this body, and that no other consideration, but the best interests of the Church, had ever induced him to advocate the organization of a new Synod, west of the Savannah river. And may I not now be permitted to reassure the brethren composing that ecclesiastical body, that they will ever have the prayers and the sympathies of the mother Synod, for their prosperity and happiness.

2. On the 10th of August, I received a note from Rev. Prof. Smeltzer, of Newberry College, inclosing therewith, a letter from the Rev. F. Hickerson, asking a dismissal from this body, to rejoin the Western Virginia Synod. As the said Western Virginia Synod had arraigned the said Hickerson for improper conduct, while yet a member of this Synod; and as Prof. Smeltzer had been appointed by this Ministerium at its last meeting, to obtain from the President

of the Western Virginia Synod, all the facts in the case of the Rev. Hickerson, to be presented for consideration at our present meeting, I hesitated for some time to comply with his request; but after mature reflection, on the 23rd of August I forwarded to him a letter of dismissal; stating simply that he had been a member of this Synod, and that at his request, he was dismissed to join the Western Virginia Synod, and no other. By this course of procedure, I have exonerated our Synod, from any obligation, touching his character, and have placed him directly under the jurisdiction of the very Synod that had preferred charges against him. As they are in possession of the facts, and not ourselves, if they receive him, they must be convinced of his innocence, if they reject him, he will then stand out of all ecclesiastical connexion, and will save us the further trouble of investigating his conduct. I sincerely hope, however, that the Western Virginia Synod, has given the brother some assurance of unimpeachable character, otherwise, he would not seek admission into a Synod, where, if guilty, he would certainly know, that his application would meet with rejection.

II. VACANCIES AND SUPPLIES.

1. In the month of December, I received a letter from the Rev. Professor Webster Eichelberger, in which he stated that he had resigned the charge of Newville Church, at Frog Level, and hoped that the people of that place would soon be supplied. Sometime, thereafter, I learned that the Rev. J. A. Sligh had accepted the charge, and has since been officiating as Pastor of said Church.

2. On the 23d of January, I received a letter from the Rev. J. D. Boozer, a member of the Mississippi Synod, in which he informed me, that the people of Orangeburg, wished him to preach in the Lutheran Church at that place, and that he had taken charge of an Academy in the vicinity from which to derive his support. I replied that I did not know what advice to give him, but supposed it could do no harm, if the people desired him to preach for them, in as much as the Synodical Missionary Society, at its last meeting, had made no provision for said Church.

3. In the month of February, I received a letter from the Rev. J. D. Stingley, of Mississippi, desiring to come to South Carolina, and wishing to know whether there were any vacant charges within the limits of this Synod? I replied that the Church in St. Stephen's parish, was the only vacancy of which I had knowledge, and I feared could not support him without other pecuniary aid. That Church is still vacant.

4. On the 19th of April, I received a letter from the Rev. D. M. Blackwelder, who stated that the Rev. Samuel Bouknight, had, from family circumstances, been compelled to resign the charge of Trinity Church, in Edgefield District, and that he had received, and accepted a call, to take charge of the same.

5. The Churches at Sandy Run, have, during the past year, been supplied with an able and efficient minister, who, I presume, will, at the present meeting, seek admission into this Synod.

6. The Rev. C. H. Bernheim informs me by letter, that two more missionaries are needed in the State of Florida, to supply the wants of our people in that region of country. I refer this matter to the consideration of the Synodical Missionary Society.

7. On the 3d Sabbath in November last, in connexion with the pastor, I dedicated the new Lutheran Church in Graniteville, S. C., which is a building of good dimensions, and well arranged for the accommodation of a large congregation. The Rev. J. N. Derrick, the first and only regular missionary to that point, now sustains himself by his own industry, independent of missionary aid. This brother has, amidst many difficulties, persevered in his exertions to build up the Church in that growing and flourishing village.

III. MISCELLANEOUS.

1. Soon after my return from Synod, I received a letter from the Rev. J. T. Bowles, of the Synod of Georgia, expressing an earnest desire to act as a general missionary to the army. I immediately addressed a letter to the Rev. A. R. Rude, one of the Committee on Army Missions, on the subject, advising him to open a correspondence with the young brother, relative to his proposition. The services of this brother were not at that time secured, and shortly afterwards, in attempting to rescue a soldier from a most perilous situation, he contracted a most malignant form of small pox, which soon terminated his useful career. His services are now lost to the Church and to the army. But the wisdom of God is unsearchable, and let us, in humble submission, bow to this dispensation of his providence.

2. In this connection, allow me to correct an erroneous impression which has, through the Southern Lutheran, as our Church organ, been made upon the public mind with reference to the Lutheran Church in the South. Correspondents from the army, and ministers and laymen at home, have all, though unintentionally, through that organ, unjustly reproached their own Church with having done nothing for the army. I must be permitted to resist this unjust sentiment, and through this report, inform the public, that the Lutheran Church in the South, has done as much in proportion to the number of her ministers, as any other denomination of Christians in the Confederacy. Our ministers and our students have gone into the ranks—have been leaders of companies—have faced danger and death, and some of them have already fallen, nobly defending their country's rights. A few have acted as chaplains, and others as missionaries to the army. But whilst, in justice to our beloved Church, I will endeavor to sustain her reputation, by correcting any erroneous impression made on the public mind, I will still by no means encourage delinquency.

3. At our last meeting, several of our clerical brethren, volunteered to go as missionaries by turns, to the army, under the direction of our Army Missionary Committee. We were pained to learn through the Southern Lutheran, that the obligation was not fulfilled, and we sincerely hope that circumstances, beyond control, have prevented its fulfillment.

4. Another class of brethren promised to go to such points of the army, and at such times, as circumstances would permit, and to do the work at their own expenses. We rejoice to learn that two of these brethren, viz: Revs. Wertz and Caughman, paid such visits to the army, and preached with success.

5. On the 26th of August, I received from the Rev. E. A. Bolles, the general agent of the Bible cause in the Confederate States of America, a full account of his labors during the years 1863 and 1864. From his report, it will be seen that this brother, has been most actively and successfully engaged, during the past two years, in his important calling. I therefore suggest to this body, the propriety of adopting some resolution, expressive of our entire confidence in the ability and fitness of the Rev. E. A. Bolles, as general agent of the Bible Society in the Confederate States of America; and that we recommend him, and the cause in which he is engaged, to all the Churches throughout his wide circuit of usefulness.

CONCLUSION.

In conclusion brethren, subjects of grave importance will no doubt come up at the present meeting for our consideration. Let each member express himself fully, but with decorum, and in the spirit of our Master. Let us seek wisdom from on high to guide us in all our deliberations; that our meeting together may exert a happy influence upon the community in which we are assembled; and the business transacted, may aid in extending the Redeemer's kingdom, and in building up the waste places of our beloved Zion. Amen.

W. BERLY, *President.*

P. S. Since completing the above report, I have received a letter from the Rev. C. H. Bernheim, stating that he was making arrangements to move to North Carolina, and could not therefore attend the present meeting of Synod; but desires a certificate of honorable dismissal from this Ministerium, to join the North Carolina Synod. In his letter, he refers to our political prospects, and the condition of our Church in the State of Florida.

W. B., *President.*

Letters and documents intended for Synod, were called for and placed in the hands of the President, for reference to the appropriate committees.

Rev. D. Sheely, excused for non-attendance at last meeting of Synod.

Synod now adjourned to meet to-morrow morning.

Prayer by Rev. C. F. Bansemer.

SECOND SESSION.

October 14th, 1864.

Synod assembled at 9 a. m., and was opened with prayer by Rev. S. Bouknight. The roll was called, the minutes of yesterday's session read and approved, when the following lay delegates having arrived, handed in their credentials, and were received as members of Synod, viz: Messrs. W. W. Housceal, Jacob Barre, Edwin King, David Nunnamaker, J. W. Dreher, J. S. Derrick and J. F. Schirmer.

The President announced the following standing committees:

1. *On Unfinished Business*—Revs. S. Bouknight and P. Derrick.
2. *On President's Report*—Revs. Prof. Smeltzer, Dr. Bachman and H. C. Franck.
3. *On Letters*—Revs. Blackwelder and J. N. Derrick.
4. *On State of Religion*—Revs. Bansemer and Rude.
5. *On Seminary Fund*—Maj. J. P. Kinard and Dr. Muller.
6. *On Synodical Fund*—Messrs. Schirmer and Wise.
7. *On Widow's Fund*—Messrs. Housceal and Zimmerman.
8. *On Memoirs*—Revs. Prof. Schreckhise and Aldrich.

Prof. Smeltzer read a letter from Rev. D. I. Dreher, Corresponding Delegate from the Synod of North Carolina, which on motion, was referred to a special Committee consisting of Rev. A. R. Rude and Dr. Muller.

At this stage of the proceedings, Rev. J. Hawkins, Corresponding Delegate of the Synod of Georgia, appeared and was welcomed to a seat as an advisory member.

Rev. Mr. Murphy and Rev. Mr. Sloan, of the Associate Reformed Church, were introduced and on motion invited to seats as advisory members.

Dr. Bachman, Chairman of the Delegation to the General Synod, read the report of said delegates, which was accepted and adopted.

REPORT OF DELEGATES TO GENERAL SYNOD.

The delegates of the Synod of South Carolina, as the General Synod of the Evangelical Lutheran Church, of the Confederate States, beg leave respectfully to report, That the Synod met pursuant to the call of the President, in Organ Church, Rowan County, North Carolina, on Thursday, May 12th, 1864. The delegates in attendance from this Synod, were, J. Bachman, D. D., Rev. Prof. Smeltzer, Rev. T. S. Boinest, Rev. A. R. Rude, Messrs. R. G. Chisolm, J. F. Schirmer, J. J. Dreher and H. C. Franck. The election for officers resulted as follows: President, Rev. A. R. Rude; Secretary, Rev. D. M. Gilbert; Treasurer, R. G. Chisolm.

The Synod was kindly received and hospitably entertained by the congregation of Organ Church; the affairs of Synod were conducted with great unanimity and order.

Preparations were made to commence the publication of the Book of Worship.

Divine service was held every day.

Rev. A. R. Rude was appointed Editor, for Southern Lutheran, for the ensuing year, and R. G. Chisolm, Financial Agent. The following resolutions were unanimously adopted by this Synod:

1*st. Resolved*, That we are more clearly than ever convinced by the barbarity and ferocity of our enemies, that it was the right and duty of the Confederate States to secede from the Union, which was intolerant and oppressive in its character.

2*nd. Resolved*, That while we most devoutly thank God, for the success which has attended our cause thus far, we fervently pray the Great Ruler of Nations, for grace to repent of the many sins, which prevent the removal of this terrible judgment from us, that we may very soon be blessed with peace and independence, and an honorable and acknowledged place among the free and independent powers of the earth.

3*rd. Resolved*, That we set the burning seal of our condemnation upon the crying sins of speculation and extortion, which are so prevalent among us, as truly outragous to humanity, and utterly incompatible with the character of any christian people.

In regard to our ecclesiastical separation from the Northern Church, the following resolution was unanimously adopted:

Resolved, That we most positively reaffirm, that while we do not desire to indulge any unchristian bitterness or uncharitableness, toward those from whom we have severed our ecclesiastical connection, it is impossible for us ever again to meet in Synodical union with those, who are urging the prosecution of this unholy war, for our subjugation and destruction.

The time and place fixed upon by the General Synod, for its next Convention, is Thursday before the third Sabbath in May, 1865, in St. John's Church, Cabarras County, North Carolina.

All of which is respectfully submitted by

J. BACHMAN, *Chairman of Delegation.*

The Corresponding Secretary presented his report. Received and adopted.

The Document placed in the hands of your Corresponding Secretary is the following, viz:

The Minutes of the 61st Convention of the Evangelical Lutheran Synod of North Carolina.

This body convened last at Mt. Carmel Church, Cabarrus County, North Carolina. It numbers sixteen Ordained Ministers and two Licentiates. Its officers are:

REV. J. CRIM, *President.*
REV. J. B. ANTHONY, *Secretary.*
REV. D. I. DREHER, *Corresponding Secretary.*
MAJ. L. J. HEILIG, *Treasurer.*

Two efficient ministers, Revs. Caleb Lentz and Joseph A. Linn, have been called to their eternal rest during the last Synodical year. A number of charges are vacant, and owing to national difficulties none are preparing for the ministry. Many of their Congregations have experienced a refreshing season of grace. These brethren are active in the work of our Blessed Master.

2. We have not received a copy of the Minutes of the Georgia Synod, and consequently can make no report. We are assured by the Delegate from the Georgia Synod, that a copy was sent to us, but are sorry that it never reached us. Respectfully submitted,

J. P. SMELTZER.

Parochial reports were called for, and the contributions to the Synodical fund.

The parochial report of each pastor was read before Synod, and in connection therewith the narratives on the State o Religion; the latter being afterward placed in the hands of the Committee on the State of Religion.

PAROCHIAL REPORT.

NAMES OF PASTORS.	Congregations.	Infants Baptized. White.	Infants Baptized. Colored.	Members Received by Baptism. White.	Baptism. Colored.	Confirmat'n. White.	Confirmat'n. Colored.	Certificate. White.	Certificate. Colored.	Dismissions. White.	Dismissions. Colored.	Communicants. White.	Communicants. Colored.	Death of Members. Adults.	Death of Members. Infants.	Prayer Meetings.	Sabbath Schools. Schools.	Sabbath Schools. Teachers.	Sabbath Schools. Scholars.	Contributions. Synod.	Contributions. Missionary Society.	Contributions. Other Societies.	Contributions. Local Objects.	Benevolent Societies.	Subscribers to Lutheran.
Rev. C. F. Bansemer..	1	28		1		1		4		18		50		2	5		1	6	45	$100 00	$ 100 00	$400 00		1	19
Rev. W. Berly........	2	2	4			2						184	4	2		1				81 85					
Rev. S. Bouknight.....	2	6		6		22	29	1		1		308	142	7		2	2	15	84	47 20	67 35				20
Rev. W. S. Bowman..	1	38	7		7	6	16			1		53	30	1	2	1	1	15	100	20 00	300 00		$1000 00		
Rev. J. N. Derrick....	1	2				1				2		35					1	9	35	23 75	2 50	2 50			8
Rev. J. B. Lowman...	3	20	23	5	3	26	3					317	105	20			1	3	23						
Rev. A. R. Rude......	1	17				15						55		9			1	4	38	135 00	182 00	82 00	200 00		
Rev. Paul Derrick....	2	11	7		6	5	16	1				136	104	5	1	2	2	8	50					1	
Rev. J. M. Schreckhise	1	11		1		2		1				78	20	5	3	1	1	6	30		46 00	2 00		1	16
Rev. J. P. Smeltzer...	1	5										50					1	8	35	20 00					15
Rev. D. Sheely.........	1	9	2	2		6						59			2										
Rev. E. Caughman....	2	6	2	8	2	10	4	1				182	8	6	2	1	2	8	45	53 00	38 00				
Rev. D. M. Blackwelder	3	12	20	2	9	36	18			2	1	330	190	19	10	3	1	6	30	170 57	20 00	100 00		2	35
Rev. A. D. L. Moser...	1	6										50		1			1	3	15	8 00	10 50		103 55	1	
Rev. J. H. Cupp......	1	10		1	3	9	2					65	48	3			1	6	25	50 00	41 00				
Rev. B. F. Berry.	3	11		6		9						112					2	11	50	10 00				1	12
Rev. W. A. Houck....	2	5	7		5		10	1		1		150	70	2			2	6	28	29 35					
Rev. A. W. Lindler....	2	5	3			5		2				114	14	2			1	5	25						
Rev. J. H. Bailey......	3	6										203	40	7	9	2	1	6	84						
Rev. B. Kreps.........	1	1			1		2		1	2		129	15	7	1					40 00					1
Rev. J. H. W. Wertz.	3	6			4	7	4					155	15	3			2	9	70	37 00					
Rev. T. S. Boinest....	3	12			3	20	6					406	20	6	5	2	3	10	120	115 00	185 00		150 00		85
Total..............	40	229	75	32	42	182	110	11	1	27	1	3216	825	107	31	13	27	144	882	$960 72	$942 35	$536 50	$1453 55	7	212

An election was entered into to fill the vacancy occasioned by the expiration of the term of the class of 1861, and the following is the present classification of the

BOARD OF DIRECTORS OF SEMINARY.

Class of 1862.	*Class of* 1863.	*Class of* 1864.
Rev. Dr. Bachman.	Rev. A. R. Rude.	Rev. D. M. Blackwelder.
Rev. S. Bouknight.	Rev. T. S. Boinest.	Rev. W. S. Bowman.
Mr. J. F. Schirmer.	Mr. H. Gallman.	Capt. J. P. Aull.
Dr. G. Muller.	Mr. W. W. Husoeal.	Capt. W. K. Bachman.

On motion the order of business was here suspended and the election of Trustees of Newberry College postponed.

The election of Delegate to Synod of North Carolina, resulted in the choice of Rev. T. S. Boinest, principal, and Rev. D. M. Blackwelder, alternate, and to the Synod of Georgia, Rev. W. S. Bowman, principal, and Rev. Prof. Smeltzer, alternate.

An election for delegates to the General Synod was now commenced, but before the result was ascertained the hour for preaching arrived, and Synod receded from business in order to give way to divine service, when Rev. G. D. Bernheim, of the Synod of North Carolina, preached from Luke xiv, 27.

Synod resumed business at the close of the religious exercises, and the tellers reported the result of the election for delegates to the General Synod as follows:

Principals.	*Alternates.*
Rev. W. Berly.	Rev. T. S. Boinest.
" N. Aldrich.	" E. A. Bolles.
" C. F. Bansemer.	" S. Bouknight.
" D. M. Blackwelder.	" E. Caughman.
" Prof. J. P. Smeltzer.	" P. Derrick.
Dr. G. Muller.	Maj. P. E. Wise.
Maj. J. P. Kinard.	Mr. H. C. Franck.
Mr. W. W. Houseal.	Mr. R. H. Zimmerman.
Mr. J. W. Dreher.	Mr. J. Barre.
Mr. F. A. Brahe.	Mr. J. H. Graman.

J. G. Houseal, Esq., presented his certificate of appointment as delegate to represent Rev. J. H. Bailey's charge, and took his seat as a member of Synod.

The following preamble and resolutions were read, and adopted by the Synod.

Inasmuch as the good order and peace of the Church, in

Augusta, has been repeatedly interrupted by the interference of a certain individual, who, though not a Lutheran minister, formerly exercised the office of its pastor, but who has been denounced by this body as an impostor,

Resolved, That even the occasional exercise of ministerial functions, in the Augusta congregation, by Mr. Meister, is hereby condemned by this Synod, and that the Vestry of the Church be requested to use their utmost endeavors to prevent said Meister from performing any ministerial act whatever in the congregation.

Resolved, That the Corresponding Secretary of this body be instructed to communicate this opinion to the Vestry of that Church.

Synod adjourned with prayer by Rev. J. B. Lowman.

THIRD SESSION.

SATURDAY MORNING, 9 A. M.

Synod convened and was opened with prayer by Rev. Prof. Eichelberger. The roll was called, the minutes read, amended and approved.

Maj. Summer read the report of the Board of Trustees of the College, which was received and adopted.

To the Evangelical Lutheran Synod of South Carolina and adjacent States :

It again devolves upon me as the organ of the Board of Trustees of Newberry College, to make an annual report of the state, condition and prospects of the College, which is placed under the care of this Board by your body.

At the meeting of the Board in January last, it was resolved by the Board to employ the Rev. J. P. Smeltzer, the President of the College, pro. tem. as the agent of the College to obtain scholarships for the College. He set out in a short time, after the adjournment of the Board, and was engaged in his work, with some intermission, till the meeting in June last, and had, by that time secured scholarships to the amount of about thirty-nine thousand dollars. The supervision of the College, and of the Subordinate Departments, was placed under the care of Prof. Robert Garlington, who immediately took charge of the College and superintended the same with efficiency and success, to the end of the session.

The number of students on the roll was sixty-seven; the attendance on the average was forty-five. The studies of the students were so arranged amongst the Professors, that all the students were regularly attended to, in the hearing of their recitations respectively.

Rev. W. Eichelberger left this State, after the commencement of the vacation, and went to Virginia as a Missionary to the Army; he has not yet returned, but is expected to be here in a few days. The other Professors are at their posts.

Owing to the difficulty of procuring board for students, which arises from the very high price of provisions and fire-wood, no students from abroad, or very few, may be expected. The Committee appointed, at the suggestion of the President of College, to make some arrangements for the securing of board for those who would be willing to come to the College, after reflecting about the matter, found it utterly impracticable. I fear it will be difficult to procure fire-wood during the winter for the rooms in the College which the students and professors occupy.

The whole number of students in the College at present are thirty; of these, four are in the College, seven in the Preparatory Department and nineteen in the Primary Department. From this it appears, that the number of students has been gradually decreasing since the commencement of this disastrous war—disastrous to the educational interests of the country; but glorious, it is to be hoped, to the cause of the Confederacy, in its final results.

The Board determined at the meeting in June, to continue the exercises of the College. This action was caused by a remark in the Report of the President of the College, that there was a rumor that the College would be suspended after the close of the session. That, if the exercises of the College were suspended, the scholarship bonds would be forfeited, and that they could not be recovered by law. This is his individual opinion, though it may not be the opinion of the Board generally.

It may not be practicable to obtain boarding this year for students: but this does not afford a good reason to suspend the exercises of the College. There are patrons of the College who have children now going to the school taught there, and will demand that this Board be ready to comply with their contract to furnish the tuition, which they bound themselves to furnish, when the bonds were given and the scholarships issued to the persons who gave bonds. There are other Colleges (Erskine College for example) whose exercises are continued, and this should afford an additional incentive not only to this Board, but to the Synod.

The altered position of affairs now, from what they were when the Board met in June, may have some influence on the Synod, in the action with reference to the College. The members of the Synod have the power to continue or to suspend the College, if they should determine as to either course, by giving instructions to the members of the Board of Trustees as to the will of Synod.

It is supposed that this matter will be brought before the Synod in the election of the Board of Trustees, and therefore the Synod ought to act with wisdom and good judgment in the matter. Should the Synod act definitely in this thing, the Secretary would bring to their notice that Erskine College is in operation ; at least so the Secretary understands by the advertisement in the newspapers, and it is worthy of consideration, whether anything will be gained by the suspension of the exercises of any of the departments of the College.

The Secretary would bring to the notice of this Synod, that the Board of Trustees recommend that a resolution be passed by this Synod, that if a member of this Board shall be absent from two successive regular meetings of this Board, such member ought not to be re-elected a member of this Board. This recommendation is made because the Board of Trustees have no power to make any such rejection.

We have the prospects of a future before us, after peace shall visit us, fraught with good not only to the College, but to the youth who may be placed under the care and instruction of the professors of the College. That there are deficiencies to be remedied is not denied; but in the present state of affairs, we think we have done as much as could be reasonably expected.

The fostering care of this Synod is imperatively demanded to promote the welfare of this College. If this Institution should be neglected by the body under whose influence it came into existence, then its prosperity will wane, and all the promises of future good which were anticipated will be disappointed. It is hoped that such is not to be the destiny of this Institution. From the interest manifested in various quarters of this State and Georgia, which our Agent, (Rev. Mr. Smeltzer,) visited during this year, we are led to the hope that this College, is to be one of those Institutions, which will hereafter exert a wholesome and beneficial influence upon those who are to fill our places long after we shall be withdrawn from the scene of our labors. We are toiling not for ourselves but for our children and for successive generations. Let our work then be well done, and thousands hereafter shall bless the day when Newberry College was founded.

Respectfully submitted,

HENRY SUMMER, *Secretary of the Board.*

Newberry College, October, 1864.

Rev. A. R. Rude made a report upon the letter of the Corresponding Delegate of the Synod of North Carolina, who was unable to attend in person.

Report received and adopted.

Your correspondent on the letter from the Delegate of the Synod of North Carolina, respectfully recommend the following preamble and resolutions:

WHEREAS, The inability of said delegate, the Rev. J. J. Dreher, to be present at the Convention of this Synod is, to its members, a cause of sincere regret, as it would have afforded us unfeigned pleasure and satisfaction to have fraternally welcomed the brother elected, not merely as the delegate from a sister Synod, but, also, as a fellow servant whom we truly love and highly respect; and, Whereas, The cordial assurance of fraternal good-will and sympathy entertained toward this Synod by the Churches of North Carolina, as, also, the earnest desire for a continuation of the friendly intercourse and harmonious co-operation now existing with this Synod on the part of the brethren, which he represents, is to us exceedingly gratifying; therefore,

Resolved, That this Synod do hereby tender to the Synod of North Carolina, its heartfelt wishes for a continuance of the favor, blessing and presence of the Great Head of the Church, as their joy is our joy, and their growth and increase is our growth and increase, as we both are but branches of the same parent tree, parts of the same great temple, even the Evangelical Lutheran Zion.

2*d Resolved*, That we sincerely regret that the delegate elected by this body failed to communicate either personally or by letter with the Synod of North Carolina.

3*d Resolved*, That this body not only desire, but will to the best of its ability, in the fear and love of God, endeavor to cultivate a continuation of the present friendly relationship existing between the two Synods.

Respectfully submitted,

A. R. RUDE.
G. MULLER.
A. H. GRAMAN.

The report of the Committee on unfinished business was read by Rev. S. Bouknight.

The Committee on Unfinished Business beg leave to present the following:

1st. There has been no report as yet from the Board of Directors of the Theological Seminary.

2d. On page 26 is a resolution requesting the Treasurer of the Widow's Fund to present the Synod, at its next meeting, with a report of the funds now in his hands.

3rd. On page 26 is a resolution requiring the Treasurer of Synod to comply with the recommendation of the Auditing Committee, on the account of the Treasurer of Synod.

4th. On page 29, is a resolution requiring every Minister and Layman to use untiring efforts to sustain the Lutheran.

5th. On page 31, is a resolution requiring every Minister in connection with this Synod to preach a sermon, and to use his influence to counteract the growing indifference to the sanctity of the Sabbath.

Respectfully submitted,

SAMUEL BOUKNIGHT.
PAUL DERRICK.

The above report was taken up by items, considered and adopted. Under item 3d, the Treasurer reported that he had not attended to the matter, in view of the depreciated condition of the currency. The whole matter was referred to the Committee on the Treasurer's Account. Under items 4th and 5th the ministers answered the interrogatories.

Rev. Prof. Smeltzer, read the report of the Committee on the President's report as follows:

REPORT ON PRESIDENT'S ADDRESS.

The Committee No. 2 on the President's Report would offer the following:

After an acknowledgement to our Heavenly Father for His gracious care over the members of Synod, and for permitting us to assemble once more in Convention; and after an allusion to the bloody drama now being enacted in our country, and the bountiful harvest with which some sections have been blessed; your President gives an account of his official acts.

1. The first item to which the President directs the attention of Synod, is, the sending of certificates of honorable dismission to the Revs. Hawkins and Austin, who have connected themselves with the Synod of Georgia. This body, in Synod assembled, would reassure these brethren, with their co-laborers, that they have our fervent prayers for their prosperity, and that we bid them a hearty God-speed in disseminating truth, and in building up the waste places of our Lutheran Zion in the growing State of Georgia.

2. The President refers to the difficulty between the Rev. F. Hickerson and the Western Virginia Synod, as it came to the notice of this body at its last session; and as the Rev. Hickerson has asked for a certificate of dismission to reunite with that body, your President gave him the certificate, hoping at the same time that he would not have asked for a dismission had not the difficulty been amicably settled. But as the Corresponding Secretary of this Synod has received an assurance from the Secretary of Western Virginia Synod, that the difficulty has been satisfactorily adjusted, no further notice need be taken of the matter.

3. The next item brought before Synod is the case of the Rev. Boozer, a Licentiate of the Mississippi Synod, taking charge of the Congregation at Orangeburg. The President seemed undecided what advice to give, but consented on the ground, that as the people desired his services, no harm would be done. In cases of this kind the Synod should express its opinion. Therefore,

Resolved, That great caution should be exercised by the presiding officer in the advice given to ministers of other Synods, and denominations, when called by our people to take charge of our congregations, and strict adherence to our discipline should be had, as a precedent might be established which would be prejudicial to the welfare of our Church.

4. The President brings to the notice of Synod, that the Rev. Cupp has taken charge of the Churches at Sandy Run. We would express our regret that the Reverend Brother could not be with us, and sympathize with him in his efforts to move his family to his place of labor, and hope by the next Convention he will be one of our number.

5. The information received, by letter, from the Rev. C. H. Bernheim, has been rightly referred to the Missionary Society.

6. The next item mentioned by the President is an erroneous impression abroad in the Church, impressed upon the public mind by correspondents in the Southern Lutheran, and repeated by Ministers and Laymen at home, that our Church has done comparatively little for the spiritual welfare of the army, and to counteract this unjust sentiment, your committee would offer the following resolutions:

Resolved, That although the Lutheran Church has not done as much as was in her power, or as was her duty, yet in comparison with the number of ministers, and the wealth of her laymen, the Lutheran Church has not been behind other denominations in their efforts to break the bread of life to our soldiers.

Resolved, That this item in the President's Report, together with these accompanying resolutions, be publ shed in the Southern Lutheran.

7. The President next brings to the notice of Synod the labor of the Rev. E. A. Bolles, General Agent of the Bible Society, during the years 1863 and 1864, in which he is engaged. Your Committee would propose the following:

Resolved, That this Synod approves of the cause in which our brother is engaged, has entire confidence in the ability of the General Agent, and heartily recommends him to the generosity of our people.

8. As a postscript the President reports that the Rev. C. H. Bernheim is making arrangements to remove into the bounds of the Synod of North Carolina, and desires a certificate of dismission from this body. Your Committee offers the following:

Resolved, That a certificate of dismission be sent to the Reverend Brother, with our prayers for his future usefulness and happiness.

In conclusion your President recommends a spirit of brotherly love, and prays that this Synod may be instrumental in building up the Kingdom of our Lord and Master. Respectfully submitted,

J. P. SMELTZER.
J. F. SCHIRMER.
H. C. FRANCKE.

The report was taken up and considered by items. Items 1st and 2d were adopted and pending the 3d item, Synod adjourned to Monday morning, 9 a. m., previously granting to Rev. S. Bouknight and Capt. D. Nunamaker, leave of absence after Sabbath services.

SABBATH SERVICES.

At 9 a. m., devotional exercises were conducted by Rev. D.

M. Blackwelder; at 10 a. m., Rev. Dr. Bachman preached to a large and attentive audience from 2 Cor. v. 17, and the followers of the Redeemer united in commemorating his dying love. After an intermission of a half hour the Congregation re-assembled, and were addressed by Rev. Prof. Smeltzer, from Psalm XXIV. 36. Thus ended the services of another Sabbath—services which will long live in the memories of many of God's people.

In the morning Rev. E. Caughman preached in the M. E. Church, at Newberry, from Luke VII. 28, and in the afternoon to the colored people of the same Church from Psalm I.

FOURTH SESSION.

MONDAY MORNING, 9 A. M.

The session of Synod was opened with prayer by Rev. J. Hawkins; the roll was called, and minutes of previous session read and adopted.

Synod resumed the consideration of the 3rd item of the report of the Committee on President's Report, and adopted it, also, items 4th, 5th, 6th, 7th and 8th, including, also, the preamble and resolutions. The report being now gone through by items, was finally adopted as a whole.

Rev. Blackwelder from the Committee on Letters, reported.

Your Committee on Letters and Excuses would report as follows:

1. Rev. B. F. Berry, gives distance and want of funds as an excuse for non-attendance at this meeting of Synod. In view of his temporal circumstances we recommend that he be excused.

2. Rev. J. P. Margart, states that his wife is too sick for him to be absent from home. We suggest that he, also, be excused. He further makes a request of protection, as a clergyman, from military duty. This we refer to the Ministerium.

3. Father J. Moser expresses an ardent wish to be with us at our present meeting, but has been hindered from age and ill health. We recommend that he be excused, and that our Synod, hereby, express the warmest sympathy in behalf of this esteemed, yet, aged and afflicted father in Israel. The same, also, we recommend in reference to father M. Rauch.

4. Rev. A. W. Lindler has a very sick child. We hope Synod will excuse him for absence.

5. Mrs. Ring, of Newberry, asks for further aid from Widow's Fund. We solicit in her behalf your continued sympathy and liberality.

Respectfully submitted,

D. M. BLACKWELDER.
J. N. DERRICK.

Revs. B. F. Berry, J. P. Margart, J. Moser, M. Rauch, A. W. Lindler, were on motion excused for not attending present meeting. Report adopted as a whole.

Rev. Bailey made a verbal excuse for Rev. Wertz. Excused.

Rev. Derrick made an excuse for Rev. Houck. Excused.

Rev. N. Aldrich was appointed to confer with the Delegate from the Synod of Georgia, in reference to a boundary line between the two Synods.

Letter from Rev. B. Kreps, giving his excuse for not attending the present meeting of Synod, was read and his excuse was sustained.

Rev. C. F. Bansemer presented the report of the Committee on the State of the Church, which was received, considered by items, and adopted as a whole.

REPORT ON THE STATE OF THE CHURCH.

In obedience to the request of Synod, the undersigned have carefully examined the reports of the brethren on the state of their respective pastorates, and we are now prepared to present the following as the result of our inquiry. The state of our Church does neither elate us, nor is it such as to give rise to any depression or despondency; for, in general, both our ministry and laity appear to be actively engaged in our Master's cause, and it would be unwise and unjust to regard the apathy of a few as a characteristic of the whole body. In relations, in which expectations were not fulfilled, it was, we are inclined to believe, owing to our inability and not to wilful neglect or indifference, that the various claims were, for the time not attended to; and the charge, "the Church has not done its duty," a crimination occasionally heard, derives its currency and popularity not so much from the agency and power of well-established truth, as from the faint light of plausibility. The Church is stationary, the attendance at public worship is small, there are but few additions to our membership, this is the language of some brethren. True, we never hear of overwhelming revivals, but may it not be the characteristic of many of our societies, what one brother predicates of his own pastorate, "the presence of the divine spirit did not manifest like a rushing mighty wind, but like the leaven hid in the meal, it worked silently, impelling the unregenerate to ask, what must we do to be saved." We have abundant cause to thank God that our state is not worse than it was before, that we hold our own, that family altars are more numerous, that the use of the means of grace is more constant; that prayer meetings are held in some, that Sabbath Schools exist in all our congregations; that the truth has been listened to with eagerness and attention, that the attendance on public worship is generally good in some, as large as it was before in others, yea even larger than in former days, and that one of our Churches in Charleston has been thronged to its utmost capacity; that in most of our communions peace prevails, and friendly relations between pastor and people; that the number of liberal laymen is increasing, that mothers and sisters are ready for every good work of benevolence and self sacrifice. That our ministers as a body sustain a fair reputation, and an unimpeached moral character. And though the prospects here and there are not bright, it affords us, nevertheless, some satisfaction to know, that the evil is owing to causes not under our control; and that both cause and effect will eventually cease to distress us, after the blessing of peace shall have returned to our land. The members of our oldest and largest congregation, in Charleston, are now dispersed over three States. But wherever they are they delight in rendering themselves useful to the cause of Christ, and though bereft in their exile of the religious privileges which they prized so highly, they are still growing in grace, wherever their venerable and beloved pastor did meet them. The same brother is actively engaged as well in promoting the bodily comfort, as in supplying the spiritual wants of the sick and wounded in our hospitals, and reports, that after careful instruction and examination he gave to 142 soldiers, certificates which will open to them the door to membership, either in the Lutheran or in any other denomination. In conclusion we would recommend that our ministers should occasionally visit our weak, languishing or newly organized congregations, to encourage pastor and people, and to assist in laying a broad and firm foundation for the growth and permanent prosperity of these pastorates. Secondly, that the pastors devote most careful attention to the religious instruction of the rising generation, by organizing not only Sunday Schools and Bible classes, but, also, by introducing more generally the rite of confirmation and its antecedent course of catechetical instruction. Thirdly, that the lay members regard it as a duty imposed upon them and their households, to attend regularly and in full representation the public worship, and encourage others by word and deed to follow their example. Fourthly, that both ministers and laymen exert themselves to increase the subscription list of the Southern Lutheran, and that the pastors regard it as an imperative obligation to increase their own usefulness, by furnishing from time to time original articles for the Lutheran. Fifthly, that our ministers preach at least once during the ensuing year on the duty of liberality and benevolence, admonishing their congregations that on account of our depreciated currency it is absolutely necessary, that they enlarge the salaries of their pastors, and increase the amount of their contributions to every charitable institution and by a prompt compliance with their promise. Some do well, but there are others who are not yet as liberal as they ought to be, either to their pastors or to the Church in general. Sixthly, that special subjects be selected for the sermons to be preached during our Synodical sessions, and that under existing circumstances, brothers Smeltzer, Boinest and the Editor of the Lutheran, arrange the matter for our next Synod.

All of which is respectfully submitted,

A. R. RUDE.
C. F. BANSEMER.

Maj. Kinard reported upon the account of the Treasurer of the Seminary. Adopted.

Dr. *Theological Seminary of Lutheran Synod of S. C., in account with* JACOB F. SCHIRMER, *Treas.* **Cr.**

1864.		
March	This amount invested in 4 per cent bonds....	$1000 00
July	Pd Rev. Smeltzer 3 q'rs salary to 1st inst ..	1125 00
October	Incidental expenses past year..............	10 00
"	Balance in hands of Treasurer..............	45 75
		$2180 75

Date	Cr.	Amount
1863		
October	Balance in hands of Treasurer,.............	$187 61
"	Received ½ year's int. on S C Railroad Bonds,	87 50
1844		
January	" 2 year's int. from Bridge Co......	45 00
February	" Interest on Harmon's Bond......	8 53
"	" Harmon's Bond in full.........	291 47
March	" Interest on Firman's Bond........	20 00
July	" 1 yrs int on A E Miller's bond to 14th May last...............	105 00
"	" 1 year's int on city 6 per cent stock	18 00
"	" 1 year's div in bank of Chester ...	275 00
"	" 1 yrs int on 4500 Con. 7 per ct b's	315 00
"	" Interest on Count's bond........	127 64
"	" Count's bond in full..............	700 00
		$2180 75
1864–Oct	Balance in hands of Treasurer..........	$45 75

SUPPLEMENTARY STATEMENT.

Personal Bonds....................................		$10879 19
Confederate 7 per cent bonds....................		4500 00
Five South Carolina Railroad 7 per cent bonds..........		2500 00
Confederate 4 per cent bonds....................		1000 00
50 half shares bank of Charleston, valued at............		2500 00
6 shares Columbia Bridge Company, "		600 00
City of Charleston 6 per cent stock.................		300 00
On deposit in Charleston Saving's Institution............	5810 28	
Interest accrued last year and now become principal.......	1289 42	7099 70
		$29378 99

The Committee appointed to examine the Report of Treasurer of the Theological Seminary, beg leave to report that they have examined the same and find it correct.

Respectfully submitted,

JOHN P. KINARD.
GERHARD MULLER.

A resolution from the Trustees of the College, asking instructions as to the course they should pursue, was presented, and in reference thereto the following was adopted:

Resolved, That the Board be recommended to continue the exercises of the College, provided, however, that no salaries be paid to the Professors except for services actually rendered, and that the Board be notified of this action.

Rev. Aldrich read the following:

The Committee appointed to confer with the Delegate from the Georgia Synod, in reference to a boundary line between that Synod and our own, would state that the Savannah river is proposed as the dividing line of the two Synods: Provided, that Churches immediately upon the line be allowed the privilege of connecting themselves with either of the two Synods, as they may prefer.

Respectfully submitted,

N. ALDRICH.

Mr. Schirmer reported upon the account of the Treasurer of Synod. Received and adopted.

DR. WM. W. HOUSEAL, *in account with the E. L. Synod of South Carolina, and adjacent States.* CR.

Date	Dr.	Amount	Date	Cr.	Amount
1863 Oct. 22.	Amount of bonds, notes and cash on hand, rising of Synod,	$2449 51	1863 Dec. 15.	Paid A. D. L. Moser, Beneficiary,	$ 25 00
	Amount received at Synod,	779 48		Balance in notes,	1322 76
1864				Interest-bearing Treasury notes,	1000 00
	Interest and principal received,	104 50		Four per cent Certificate,	700 00
				Cash,	285 73
		$3333 49			$3333 49

NOTES AND BONDS IN HANDS OF TREASURER.

Bond of Ed. Harmon,	for $	32 95	with interest from	February, 1860
Note of H. Summers,	for	200 00	"	January, 1861
" D. I. Dreher,	for	200 00	"	October, 1858
" J. Kleckly,	for	200 00	"	November, 1860
" Rev. J. H. Bailey,	for	305 00	"	October, 1859
" S. W. Boozer,	for	181 31	"	October, 1860
" J. S. Lewis,	for	50 20	"	October, 1860
" Rev. B. Kreps,	for	50 00	"	October, 1862
" D. Kleckley,	for	34 90	"	October, 1860
" J. L. Meetze,	for	30 00	"	November, 1860
" Elijah Wingard,	for	31 85	"	October, 1860
" Rev. J. H. Bailey,	for	6 50	"	April, 1859
		$1322 76		

The Committee to whom were referred the accounts of the Treasurer of Synod, beg leave to report: That they have discharged the duty assigned to them and find the accounts correct, but regret the Treasurer has not complied with the Resolution of last year, and would again earnestly recommend that the Resolution be carried out. The Committee would further recommend to the Treasurer that in future in making out his account, he would specify particularly from what sources he receives either Principal or interest. The present assets in his hands are:

Personal notes and Bonds, - -	1322 76
Interest bearing Treasury Notes, - -	1000 00
Certificates of 4 per cent Bonds, - -	700 00
Cash in hands, - - - - - -	285 73
	$3308 49

Annexed is a statement of Bonds. Respectfully submitted,

JACOB F. SCHIRMER, } Committee.
P. E. WISE, }

The report of the Committee on Memoirs was read by Prof. Schreckhise, the Chairman, and adopted by the Synod rising and in silence.

MEMOIR ON THE DEATH OF MR. JOHN H. McCULLOUGH, RECENTLY A STUDENT OF OUR THEOLOGICAL SEMINARY.

The subject of this memoir, Mr. J. H. McCollough, was born in Newberry District, So. Ca. He professed faith in Christ, and joined the Church at Beth Eden, during the ministry of Rev. J. Hawkins. He afterwards entered the College at Newberry, and then the Theological Seminary. Possessed of a good understanding, which had been improved by diligent application, and above all being a man of devoted piety, he gave promise of great usefulness in the Church, had he lived to become an embassador of Christ. He had not entered upon the active duties of the ministry, but was almost prepared to assume those duties, when he was summoned by his country to enter her service as a soldier. He preserved his christian integrity amidst all the temptations of camp life, and ever "adorned the doctrines of our Saviour by a consistent walk and godly conversation." He was killed by a shell, on the field of battle, near Spottsylvania, Court House, on the twelfth of May, 1864. Faithful during life in the discharge of all his Christian duties, he died in the full triumphs of a living faith in Christ. His death appeals to us, all ministers, to be, also, ready, and teaches the truth, that as a Church we should be deeply engaged in praying to the Lord of the harvest, that He would send forth laborers in his Vineyard.

Respectfully submitted,

J. M. SCHRECKHISE.
N. ALDRICH.

Ordered that a copy of the above be furnished to the nearest relations, and that it be published in the Southern Lutheran.

Revs. Dr. Bachman, W. S. Bowman and Dr. G. Muller, were appointed to express, through the Southern Lutheran, our sympathies with our suffering people.

The following resolutions were adopted:

Resolved, That the Treasurer of the Widow's Fund be requested to pay over to Mrs. Cloy, Mrs. Ring and Mrs. Leppard, each the sum of fifty dollars for the ensuing year.

Resolved, That the proceedings of the Missionary Society, also, the account current of the Widow's Fund Society, be appended to our Minutes.

Resolved, That our Delegate to the next meeting of the North Carolina Synod, be requested to make some inquiry as to the resolution passed by that body, concerning some money which was ordered to be paid over to our Seminary Fund.

Resolved, That the Treasurer of the Widow's Fund, be requested to collect some of the assets that he may have in his possession, so that he may meet the orders made upon, and the balance due him by said fund.

Resolved, That at the close of the public services of this day the thanks of this Synod be tendered to the friends of this neighborhood, and the members of this Church for their unremitted kindness and attention to us during our sojourn among them, and the assurance that they have our prayers and wishes that in the midst of all the troubles now surrounding them, God in his mercy may spare to them those who are dear to them, and are now absent from them.

Synod took a recess for divine service, when Rev. P. Derrick preached from Psalm rx, 10.

After divine service Synod resumed business, and the report of the Directors of Seminary was read and adopted.

REPORT OF THE BOARD OF DIRECTORS OF THE THEOLOGICAL SEMINARY.

The assembling of another ecclesiastical convention, reminds the Board, that they are expected to make to the Synod a report of the condition of the Institution, over whose interests they have been appointed guardians; and would that they could as in days of yore tell you of bright prospects, and high hopes of a rapid increase of our ministry, and hence of large measures to be set on foot for the extension of the mother of Protestantism, and the building up of the Church of the Redeemer. But, alas, here too, as in every other department of the Church, the blighting effects of this cruel war have been too keenly felt, and we mourn over the demise of many of those, who, in course of preparation gave promise of great usefulness in the vineyard of the Master.

By the demands made of the young men of the country, our Seminary walls are deserted of her students, and without any prospect of their return until this fratricidal strife shall be terminated. But your Professor has not been idle—his energies and time have been devoted to the interests of the College, from the Trustees of which he, with the consent of this Board, has accepted an agency for fully endowing the College, and is thus subserving the future interest of the Seminary.

T. S. BOINEST, *Secretary of Board.*

Resolved, That the Treasurer of Seminary be requested to settle with our Professor, the salary that may be due him at the period when the same became due.

Report on the Account of Treasurer of Widow's Fund, read and adopted.

Widow's Fund of Lutheran Synod of South Carolina, in account with John P. Kinard, *Treasurer.*

DR.

1860	Paid Dr. Bachman for Mrs. Ring, - - - - -	$50 00
1864 Oct	" Mrs. Ring, - - - - - - - -	50 00
1863 Oct	" Mrs. Cloy, for two years, - - - - -	100 00
"	" Mrs. Leppard for two years, - - - - -	100 00
1862 Jan	Loaned Jacob Kibler on note, - - - -	1100 00
		$1400 00
1864 Oct	Balance due Treasurer, - - - - - -	$241 00

CR.

1862 Jan	Received amount of Vaughan's Bond in July, -	$1000 00
"	" interest on the above, - - - - -	159 00
	Balance due Treasurer, - - - - - - - -	241 00
		$1400 00

ASSETS IN HANDS OF TREASURER.

Note of Rev. E. Dufford	for $40 00	with interest from	October 1857
" " J. H. Bailey	for 21 07	"	Novem 1857
Bond of " "	for 100 00	"	October 1860
" A. G. Summer	for 1122 53	"	Novem 1860
Note of Jacob Kibler	for 1100 00	"	January 1862
	$2293 60		

The Committee appointed to audit the accounts of the Treasurer of the Widow's Fund, report, that they find it correct, and payments properly vouched. Appended is a supplementary statement showing the assets in his hands, consisting of notes and bonds, to be twenty-two hundred and ninety-three dollars and sixty cents.

Respectfully submitted, W. W. HOUSEAL.

The Treasurer read the following statement of contributions to Synodical fund :

SYNODICAL CONTRIBUTIONS.

Rev. Samuel Bouknight's charge—		
Macedonia,	$20 00	
St. Mark's,	27 20—	$ 47 20
Rev. W. S. Bowman's charge—		
Morris Street,		20 00
Rev. C. F. Bansemer's charge—		
German Evangelical-Lutheran Church, Augusta, Ga.,		100 00
Rev. D. M. Blackwelder's charge—		
St. Michael's,	68 50	
St. Paul's,	76 65	
Trinity,	30 00—	175 15
Rev. B. F. Berry's charge—		
Mt. Pleasant,		11 35
Rev. W. Berly's charge—		
St. Stephen's,	48 00	
St. Andrew's,	33 85—	81 85
Rev. T. S. Boinest's charge—		
Bethlehem,	45 00	
St. Luke's,	40 00	
St. John's,	30 00—	115 00
Rev. J. H. Bailey's charge—		
St. Mathew's,	17 75	
Colony,	44 95	
Liberty Hill,	10 00—	72 70
Rev. E. Caughman's charge—		
Good Hope,	6 00	
Nazareth,	40 00—	46 00
Rev. J. N. Derrick's charge—		
St. James',		23 75
Rev. Paul Derrick's charge—		
St. Mathew's and Mount Lebanon,		90 70
Rev. J. H. Cupp's charge—		
Sandy Run,		50 00
Rev. W. A. Houck's charge—		
Pine Grove and Trinity,		27 95
Rev. A. W. Lindler's charge—		
St. John's,	14 00	
Mt. Zion,	13 55—	27 55
Rev. A. R. Rude's charge—		
Ebenezer, Columbia,		155 00

Rev. Dr. Bachman's charge—		
St. John's, Charleston,		179 25
Rev. J. B. Lowman's charge—		
St. David's,	27 00	
St. Peter's,	15 60	
Bethel,	35 00—	77 60
Rev. Prof. Smeltzer's charge—		
Luther Chapel,		20 00
Rev. Prof. Schreckhise's charge—		
Beth Eden,		164 00
Rev. A. D. L. Moser's charge—		
Mt. Zion,		8 50
Rev. J. A. Sligh's charge—		
Newville,		25 00
Rev. B. Kreps' charge—		
Mt. Calvary,		40 00
Rev. J. H. W. Wertz's charge—		
Salem,	5 30	
Union,	9 70	
Corinth,	22 00—	37 00
		1595 55
Deduct uncurrent bills,		7 75
Total.		$1587 80

Election of Trustees of College resulted as follows:

Rev. Dr. Bachman.	L. J. Jones.
" A. R. Rude.	J. K. Schumpert.
" T. S. Boinest.	Capt. J. P. Aull.
" D. M. Blackwelder.	H. Summer.
" W. S. Bowman.	N. A. Hunter.
" S. Bouknight.	Gen. A. C. Garlington.
Dr. G. Muller.	Dr. O. B. Mayer.
W. K. Bachman.	Col. S. Fair.
Silas Johnstone.	Maj. J. P. Kinard.

St. Mathew's Church, Orangeburg, So. Ca., was selected as the next place of meeting, and Thursday, before 3rd Sabbath in October, 1865, the time.

Resolved, That hereafter, it shall be contrary to our discipline, for any Vestry or Church council to permit a minister of another denomination to officiate regularly in any Church or pastorate within the bounds of this Synod, and the Church councils of such Churches, are, hereby, instructed to prevent any such occupation of our Churches and pulpits, as calculated to produce disturbance and tending to destroy the Churches.

Resolved, That the Corresponding Secretary be instructed to communicate this resolution to such Church Council.

Resolved, That 500 copies of the Minutes of this session be printed under superintendance of Secretary.

Resolved, That the Secretary be authorized to notify the Treasurer, previous to the printing of the Minutes, of the necessity of having the funds ready for the payment of the same, so that there may be no disappointment in settling with the printer.

The following action was taken in reference to the establishment of a second English Lutheran Church, in the city of Charleston :

WHEREAS, The establishment of a second English Lutheran Church, in Charleston, has for a long time been a cherished object of this body. And, whereas, the only impediment in the way, of the speedy consummation of this object, is the inadequacy of our present Church edifice, therefore,

Resolved, That the agent of this corporation be invited to visit our pastorates and make collections, so as to be prepared to build a suitable house of worship so soon as the war shall have ended.

Ordered, That if there be any unfinished business it be referred to the Ministerium.

Resolved, That Synod now adjourn to meet at the time and place above specified.

The exercises were closed with appropriate religious exercises conducted by the Rev. Dr. Bachman.

THADDEUS STREET BOINEST,
Secretary of Synod of South Carolina.

Minutes of the Ministerium.

FIRST SESSION.

Beth Eden Church, October 13th, 1864.

The ministerium assembled this morning and was opened with prayer by Rev. J. B. Lowman.

The Sermons and Journals of Revs. Moser and Sligh, licentiates, were called for and referred to a committee consisting of Revs. N. Aldrich and P. Derrick.

Rev. N. Aldrich presented the following preamble and resolution which were unanimously adopted:

Whereas, There are reports in circulation unfavorable to the ministerial character of Rev. A. Angerer, therefore,

Resolved, That a committee be appointed to investigate these charges, and to report as early as practicable to the President of this Synod.

The following were appointed the committee: Revs. L. Muller, Dr. Bachman and Bowman.

Adjourned with prayer by Rev. J. N. Derrick.

SECOND SESSION.

Ministerium was opened in the usual manner; and the following report of the Committee on Sermons and Journals was read by Rev. N. Aldrich and adopted:

REPORT OF THE COMMITTEE ON SERMONS AND JOURNALS.

Your Committee would report that the papers placed in their hands, were the Sermons and Journals of Rev. A. D. L. Moser and Rev. J. A. Sligh. As regards the sermons of these young brethren, we cannot but express ourselves as highly gratified in their perusal. They are not only systematically arranged, but their respective themes have been discussed in accordance with sound doctrine and practical piety. The indications are, that by continued efforts, under the guidance of the Holy

Spirit, these brethren will become skillful workmen in the vineyard of the Lord.

Their Journals show them to have been constantly and actively employed in their ministerial duties during the past Synodical year.

We recommend a renewal of the Licenses of these young brethren for another year. Respectfully submitted,

N. ALDRICH,
PAUL DERRICK.

A letter was read from the Secretary of the Western Virginia Synod, stating that they had examined into the charges against Rev. F. Hickerson, and the result arrived at was that Rev. Hickerson had not been guilty of any moral delinquency, but the difficulties had arisen from a misunderstanding now impossible, in consequence of death, to remove.

Ministerium then adjourned.

THADDEUS STREET BOINEST,
Secretary of Ministerium of South Carolina.

Minutes of Missionary Society.

BETH EDEN, Saturday October 15th, 1864.

The Society met this morning at 10 o'clock, and the annual sermon was preached by Rev. A. R. Rude. The business session was opened with prayer by Rev. W. S. Bowman. The President, Mr. J. F. Schirmer, in the chair, announced the terms of membership and appointed a committee to receive contributions. A proposition was also made for subscribers of $100, and $50 each, and the following was reported as the result:

INDIVIDUAL CONTRIBUTIONS.

Dr. G. Muller,	$100 00	Mrs. J. C. Sligh,	$5 00
Maj. J. P. Kinard,	100 00	Mrs. J. G. Houseal,	5 00
Jacob Barre,	100 00	Rev. A. W. Lindler,	5 00
R. Zimmerman,	100 00	Rev. J. A. Sligh,	5 00
Capt. Aull,	100 00	Mrs. T. S. Boinest,	5 00
D. Nunnamaker,	100 00	Miss A. V. Boinest,	5 00
F. A. Brahe,	100 00	H. Summer, Esq.,	5 00
J. S. Long,	100 00	J. L. Cromer,	5 00
F. Muller,	100 00	Dr. G. W. Glenn,	5 00
Rev. E. Caughman,	100 00	Rev. Prof. Schreckhise,	5 00
H. W. Rikard,	100 00	Mrs. Schreckhise,	5 00
Rev. A. R. Rude,	50 00	A. G. Dickert,	5 00
Rev. T. S. Boinest,	50 00	J. A. Kibler,	5 00
R. G. Chisolm,	50 00	W. W. Houseal,	5 00
Rev. Dr. Bachman,	50 00	R. H. Zimmerman,	5 00
Maj. P. E. Wise,	50 00	Mrs. Zimmerman,	5 00
J. H. Graman,	50 00	Mrs. Gen. Kinard,	5 00
J. F. Schirmer,	10 00	Mrs. M. M. D'Oyley,	5 00
Miss A. R. Kibler,	10 00	Mrs. F. Holman,	5 00
M. Isehour,	10 00	Rev. D. M. Blackwelder,	5 00
Rev. W. Eichelberger,	10 00	Mrs. Blackwelder,	5 00
J. G. Houseal,	10 00	Rev. J. P. Smeltzer,	5 00
T. Chandler,	10 00	Mrs. Smeltzer,	5 00
D. Wicker,	10 00	Miss C. E. Aull,	3 25
Mrs. M. Baker,	10 00	Mrs. W. S. Bowman,	4 00
John Glasgow,	10 00	Rev. D. Sheely,	3 50
J. W. Dreher,	10 00	Mrs. E. R. McKellar,	3 00
Mrs. E. L. Aull,	6 50	Rev. A. D. L. Moser,	3 00
Miss Betty Epting,	5 00	Rev. E. Caughman,	3 00

Rev. W. A. Houck,	$2 50	Mrs. E. M. McMorries,	$1 00
Mrs. Houck,	2 50	Miss M. Strobel,	1 00
Mrs. S. A. Bailey,	2 50	R. W. D. Sligh,	1 00
Miss L. Bailey,	2 50	Mrs. M. D. Haigler,	1 00
Mrs. A. C. Strobel,	2 50	Mrs. J. Glasgow,	1 00
Mrs. L. Sheely,	2 00	Mrs. M. Sligh,	1 00
Rev. J. N. Derrick,	2 00	Mrs. M. P. Thomson,	1 00
Mrs. S. C. Derrick,	2 00	Rev. E. A. Bolles,	1 00
Mrs. C. Glasgow,	2 00	Mrs. A. A. Bolles,	1 00
Mrs. D. Hunter,	2 00	Miss F. Bolles,	1 00
Mrs. H. Summer,	2 00	Mrs. E. B. Bull,	1 00
Mrs. Sarah A. Bolles,	2 00	Miss M. D. Bull,	1 00
Mrs. E. Summer,	2 00	H. E. Bull,	1 00
J. G. Rikard,	2 00	Mrs. E. Hunter,	1 00
Rev. W. S. Bowman,	2 00	Mrs. C. Greneker,	1 00
Mrs. W. Riser,	2 00	Mrs. A. D. Strobel,	1 00
A. King,	2 00	Miss L. Hunter,	75
J. Setzler,	2 00	W. A. Rikard,	1 00
J. B. Fellers,	2 00	J. S. Derrick,	1 00
W. R. Hentz,	2 00	Rev. W. Berly,	1 00
Q. N. Berly,	2 00	Mrs. N. Aull,	1 00
Mrs. E. C. Berly,	2 00	Dr. D. E. McMorries,	1 00
Mrs. L. E. Glymph,	2 00	Mrs. Sarah Smith,	2 00
Rev. J. Moser,	2 00	Miss E. Folk,	1 00
Mrs. E. F. J. Moser,	2 00	Miss M. L. Chandler,	1 00
Mrs. E. Caughman,	2 00	Mrs. C. Folk,	1 00
Rev. S. Bouknight,	2 00	Mrs. N. Sligh,	1 00
Rev. P. Derrick,	2 00	Master McMorries,	50
Mrs. A. B. Derrick,	2 00	Rev. J. H. W. Wertz,	1 00
Mrs. J. McMorries,	1 00		

LIFE MEMBERS.

Maj. P. E. Wise,	$20 00	Jacob Barre,	$20 00
F. A. Brahe,	20 00	Miss M. Wilbur,	20 00

CONGREGATIONAL CONTRIBUTIONS.

Rev. P. Derrick's charge, St. Mathew's and Mount Lebanon		$ 53 00
Rev. Prof. Smeltzer's charge, Luther Chapel,		38 35
Rev. J. B. Lowman's charge, St. Peter's,		11 oo
Rev. S. Bouknight's charge, St. Mark's,		67 35
Rev. W. Berly's charge, St. Stephen's,	$13 45	
St. Andrew's,	22 oo—	35 45
Rev. B. F. Berry's charge, Mt Pleasant,		15 7o
Rev. A. D. L. Moser's charge, Mt. Zion,		10 5o
Rev. D. Sheely's charge, Bethlehem,		14 oo
Rev. Dr. Bachman's charges, Sabbath School Sewing Society,		70 25
" Sabbath School,		3o oo
" Ladies' Society,		12 5o
Rev. D. M. Blackwelder's charge, St. Michael's		2o oo

Rev. A. R. Rude's charge, Ebenezer, Columbia, : :		100 00
" Sabbath School, : :		30 25
Rev. W. S. Bowman's charge, Morris St., Lutheran Church,		300 00
Rev. Prof. Shreckhise's charge, Beth Eden, : :		46 00
Rev. E. Caughman's charge, Good Hope, :	7 50	
Nazareth, : :	32 35—	39 85
Rev. J. H. Cupp's charge, Sandy Run, : : :		41 00
Rev. C. F. Bansemer's charge, Augusta Church, : :		100 00
Rev. J. A. Sligh's charge, Newville, : : :		25 00
Rev. T. S. Boinest's charge, Bethlehem, : :	72 80	
St. Luke's, : :	60 38	
St. John's, : :	52 00—	185 18

Recapitulation.

Individual contributions, : :	$1,747 00
Life members, : : :	80 00
Congregational contributions, : :	1,245 20
	$3,072 20

The officers of the preceding year were unanimously re-elected, and Mr. J. W. Dreher appointed assistant Treasurer, in view of the Treasurer elect being absent in the army.

President—J. F. Schirmer.

Vice-Presidents—Revs. Dr. Bachman, W. S. Bowman, and Major J. P. Kinard.

Recording Secretary—Rev. T. S. Boinest.

Corresponding Secretary—Rev. D. M. Blackwelder.

Treasurer—Mr. J. J. Dreher.

Executive Committee—Revs. J. P. Smeltzer, J. M. Schreckhise, T. S. Boinest, Messrs. W. W. Houseal, M. Barre, J. P. Kinard, and J. J. Dreher.

The Corresponding Secretary presented the following report which was received and adopted:

REPORT OF CORRESPONDING SECRETARY OF MISSIONARY SOCIETY.

In accordance with a requirement found on page 41, of the minutes of last year, your Corresponding Secretary at an early date addressed letters of inquiry to our missions in Florida. After many months had elapsed letters were received from both missions, to the effect that, as far as could be seen, there was no probability of building up our Church in that section while this war continues, and that we as a Church would better combine our resources in support of army missions.

During last July an earnest application was made to your Executive Committee to support Rev. W. A. Julian, a worthy young brother from the North Carolina Synod, who had gone to labor in our Florida Mission field. The Executive Committee met, and having duly considered the application, resolved to give brother Julian $30 per month, provided, he expressed it his intention to labor in this field at least two or three years, otherwise the Committee felt unwilling to give any support. This action was immediately communicated to brother Julian; but no answer thereto has been received.

Your Corresponding Secretary has learned from a letter addressed to brother Berly, President of our Synod, that our former Missionary, Rev. C. H. Bernheim, and, also, Rev. W. A. Julian, are fleeing from Florida to North Carolina, as refugees, to escape the horrors of Yankee rule. Rev. J. H. Mengert is still in Florida, and makes application to your Society for pecuniary aid. Our military and ecclesiastical prospects in Florida are most gloomy, indeed desperate, and in view of all known circumstances, your Corresponding Secretary suggests that this mission field be abandoned until a brighter day dawn upon that land of flowers.

Our esteemed Missionary at Charleston, Rev. W. S. Bowman, has reported regularly. His labors have abounded, having preached 87 times during the past year, and attended faithfully to all the other duties of a successful ministry. In spite of bomb shells and all other annoyances his labors have been blessed. Thronging multitudes wait upon his ministrations. Piety and liberality are becoming more and more manifest. Indeed all the elements of a strong, self-ruling, and influential Church are operating, and unless counteracted by this desolating war will, eventually, fully develop themselves. We commend this Mission and its Missionary to your continued sympathy, your liberality and your prayers, and to the prayers of all our Churches. D. M. BLACKWELDER.

Treasurer's report was received and handed to the following Auditing Committee: Dr. G. Muller, R. H. Zimmerman.

Resolved, That all surplus monies be paid over to the Treasurer of Army Mission Fund.

Resolved, That five hundred dollars be appropriated to the Church in Charleston.

Resolved, That in the expenditure of the funds contributed by this Society, army Chaplains are to have the preference over Missionaries.

The Committee appointed to audit the account of the Treasurer of the Society made a report as follows:

JOHN J. DREHER, *Treasurer, in account with Synodical Missionary Society of the Evangelical Lutheran Synod of South Carolina and adjacent States.*

1863	DR.	
Oct 20	To balance in cash as per report rendered at Synod held in Bethlehem Church, Newberry District, S. C.	$226 03
	To whole amount of contributions received at Synod held as above stated	1170 30
Dec 4	By amount of H. D's bond paid in full	144 00
"	By interest in full on said bond,	10 81
		$1551 14

1863	CR.	
Oct 19	To cash paid Rev. B. Kreps,	$100 00
" 21	" " Rev. W. S. Bowman,	300 00
1864		
Feb 24	To cash sent Rev. W. S. Bowman,	250 00
Oct 15	Balance in hands of Treasurer,	901 14
		$1551 14

Oct 15	Balance in hands of Treasurer	$901 14
"	Amount of Note in hand	16 14
"	" on deposit in Saving's Institution,	201 36
		$1118 64

JOHN J. DREHER, Treasurer.

The committee appointed to examine the account of the Treasurer of Synodical Missionary Society, ask leave to report. That they have examined the same and find the account correct, and the payments properly vouched.

Respectfully submitted, GERHARD MULLER.
RUSSEL H. ZIMMERMAN.

Received and adopted.

Resolved, That the Synod be requested to publish the Minutes of this Society in connection with theirs.

Rev. A. D. L. Moser was appointed to preach the next anniversary sermon, and Rev. J. A. Sligh be his alternate.

Adjourned with prayer by Rev. S. Bouknight.

T. STREET BOINEST,
Secretary Missionary Society.

SOCIETY FOR THE RELIEF OF DISABLED MINISTERS, ETC.

The following donations for the funds of this Society were received at this session of Synod:

Sunday School Society of Charleston,	70 25
Mr. F. Muller,	10 00
Miss C Bachman,	10 00
Sunday School, Columbia Church,	32 00
J. F. Schirmer,	5 00
Miss Lovegreen,	3 00
Miss A. D. Strobel,	2 50
In part per Rev. E. A. Bolles, to constitute Mrs. Bolles a life member,	10 00
Total,	$142 75

Society for Relief of Disabled Ministers, etc., in account with F. C. Blum, *Treasurer.*

DR.

1864	Apr	Deposited in Saving's Institution,	$81 00
			$81 00

CR.

1863	Oct	Balance in hands of Treasurer,	$00 19
"	Oct	Received at session of Synod this date,	80 00
1864	Oct	Balance due Treasurer,	00 81
			$81 00

ASSETS IN HANDS OF TREASURER.

Bond of Rev. C. H. Bernheim, dated Feb. 18, 1858 with interest from October, 1861,		$625 00
Amount on deposit in Saving's Institution,	$1,296 24	
Interest accrued past year not drawn, now principal,	219 12	—1515 36
		$2,140 36

MINUTES

OF THE

Evangelical L. Synod and Ministerium,

SYNODICAL MISSIONARY SOCIETY,

AND OF

The Society for the Relief of Disabled Ministers.

1865.

MINUTES OF SYNOD.

FIRST SESSION.

St. Mathews' Church, Orangeburg Dist., Oct. 12, 1865.

The Evangelical Lutheran Synod of South Carolina, and adjacent States, convened at St. Mathews' Church, Orangeburg District, S. C., this morning at 11 o'clock, and the opening sermon was preached by the President, Rev. W. Berly, from Psalm cxxxiii, 1.

The Synodical session was opened with an appropriate hymn and a prayer by the President, when the roll was called and the following ministers answered to their names:

Ordained Ministers.

1. Rev. J. Bachman, D. D. .... Charleston, S. C.
2. " W. Berly .... Lexington, S. C.
3. " E. A. Bowles** .... Orangeburg "
4. " T. S. Boinest .... Pomaria, "
5. " S. Bouknight .... Leesville, Lex. District, "
6. " P. Derrick .... St. Mathews, "
7. " J. N. Derrick .... Graniteville, "
8. " E. Dufford .... Fort Motte, "
9. " W. A. Houck .... Orangeburg, "
10. " A. W. Lindler .... Germanville, "
11. " Prof. J. P. Smeltzer .... Newberry, "
12. " J. H. W. Wertz .... Frog Level, "
13. " J. H. Cupp† .... Sandy Run, "

Licentiates.

1. Rev. A. D. L. Moser .... Pomaria, S. C.
2. " J. A. Sligh .... Frog Level, "

**General Agent of Bible Society for South Carolina.

†Received at this session.

Ordained Ministers Absent.

1. Rev. N. Aldrich....................................Charleston, S. C.
2. " J. H. Bailey....................................Frog Level, "
3. " C. F. Bansemer....................................Augusta, Ga.
4. " B. F. Berry‖....................................Cowpen Branch, S. C.
5. " D. M. Blackwelder‖....................................Pomaria, "
6. " W. S. Bowman*....................................Charleston, "
7. " E. Caughman‖....................................Frog Level, "
8. " Prof. W. Eichelberger‖....................................Cantonsville, Md.
9. " B. Kreps*....................................Edisto Mills, S. C.
10. " J. B. Lowman....................................Lexington, C. H., "
11. " J. P. Margart....................................Eufaula, Ala.
12. " J. Moser‖....................................Hope Station, S. C.
13. " L. Muller....................................Charleston,.... "
14. " M. Rauch‖....................................Germanville, "
15. " A. R. Rude....................................Columbia, "
16. " Prof. J. M. Schreckhise‖....................................Mt. Sidney, Va.
17. " D. Sheely‖....................................Rockville, S. C.
18. " F. Wilkin....................................

*Appeared after first session.

‖Excused.

The certificates of the lay delegates were called for, and the names of the following were registered as members of Synod:

Lay Delegates.

R. G. Chisolm..................	from	Rev.	Dr. Bachman's	charge.
Capt. W. G. Metts..............	"	"	T. S. Boinest's	"
P. E. Wise.....................	"	"	S. Bouknight's	"
J. D. Kellar, Esq..............	"	"	P. Derrick's	"
D. J. Zeigler...................	"	"	W. A. Houck's	"
J. S. Derrick..................	"	"	A. W. Lindler's	"
J. J. Rauch....................	"	"	J. H. W. Wertz's	"
S. P. Dickard..................	"	"	A. D. L. Moser's	"
J. D. Sease, Esq...............	"	"	B. F. Berry's	"
H. W. Rikard	"	Both Eden,		"

Revs. A. R. McCorquadale and J. D. W. Crook, of the M. E. Church South, were introduced and invited to seats as advisory members.

The Delegates to the General Synod stated that there had been no meeting of that body, and consequently they had no report to make.

The Delegate appointed to the meeting of the North Carolina Synod, reported that he received information from a member of that body, that there would be no meeting of that Synod, in consequence of the disturbed state of the country, consequently he did not attend to his assigned duty.

The President next read his annual report, which was received and laid on the table for reference to a committee.

PRESIDENT'S ANNUAL REPORT.

Beloved Brethren:

Another year has passed away since we last met together in a Synodical capacity; and now we are assembled under peculiar circumstances, yet we have reason to be thankful to the Father of all our mercies, that the lives of all the clerical members, composing this ecclesiastical body, have been spared; and that we are not called upon to mourn the loss, by death, of a single brother in the ministry. From the casualties of war, and the locality of your presiding officer, he has, since the middle of February last, been cut off from the outward world; having no communication by mail with any part of our beloved Church; a few letters, however, reached him by chance.

I. OFFICIAL.

1. On the 6th of December, I received a communication from the Rev. C. H. Bernheim, of Florida, (who had applied for a letter of dismissal from this body previous to its last meeting, with a view of connecting himself with the Evangelical Lutheran Synod of South Carolina,) stating that he would remain in that country for the present, but desired to connect himself with the Evangelical Lutheran Synod of Georgia, I immediately forwarded to him, at his request, the necessary credentials.

2. In the month of January, last, I received from the Rev. J. H. Cupp, of Sandy Run, his certificate of dismissal from the Virginia Synod, to connect himself with this body, which I herewith present. Brother Cupp was to have united with us at our last annual meeting, but was prevented from doing so, from unavoidable circumstances.

3. On the 6th of July, I received a letter from the Rev. T. S. Boinest, Secretary of Synod, inclosing an application from the Rev. A. Angerer, of Walhalla, for dismission from this Synod, to connect himself with the Synod of Maryland. A few days thereafter I forwarded to him the desired certificate.

II. VACANCIES AND SUPPLIES.

1. About the time of our last annual meeting, the Rev. Prof.

James M. Schreckhise, of Newberry College, resigned the pastoral charge of Beth Church, in Newberry District, S. C.; to which, in connexion with St. Mathew's and Liberty Hill Churches, which formed the original pastorate, the Rev. Jacob Hawkins, of the Evangelical Lutheran Synod of Georgia, received, and accepted a call, and entered upon his official duties in the month of January last.

Professor Schreckhise, in consequence of the partial suspension of the College at Newberry, has since that period removed to Virginia, where it is hoped, he is now, successfully and usefully engaged.

2. I know of no churches vacant at present, within the limits of this Synod, except the Church in St. Stephen's Parish; which has been in a destitute condition for several years past; and the Church in Orangeburg Village.

Since writing the above, I have received a letter from the Rev. D. M. Blackwelder, stating that he had resigned the charge of Trinity Church, in Edgefield District, and St. Michael's in Lexington District; and, also, a letter from the Rev. J. N. Derrick, informing me that he had resigned his charge at Graniteville, S. C.

III. MISCELLANEOUS.

1. Our Theological and literary institutions at Newberry, have been in a languishing condition for the past three years, in consequence of the dreadful war that has scourged the land. All our Theological students proper, as well as those preparing for the ministry, have either fallen upon the battle field, or died from disease; not one has escaped.

The Theological Seminary then, has, from unavoidable circumstances, closed itself; and it must be left to the judgment of those who manage the College and preparatory departments, whether the exercises in these institutions shall be suspended for the present, or not.

IV. CONCLUSION.

Brethren, subjects of the most momentous consequences, that have ever engaged the attention of this body, will present themselves at the present meeting, for our consideration. Men will always differ on subjects of any grave importance, but let each one, whilst he shall be permitted to express himself, fearlessly, fully, fairly and honestly, so regard the opinions of his brethren, that no undue temper shall be manifested, but that we may keep the unity of the spirit in the bonds of peace.

My term of office has now expired, and I avail myself of the present opportunity, of expressing to you my sincere thanks, for the confidence you have reposed in me; and I now return to you the sacred trust which you committed to me, with the earnest desire that you will confer this honor upon another. With my impaired health, and the difficulties that surrounded me, I have endeavored to discharge the duties of my office to the best of my ability. And now, brethren, may peace, prosperity and happiness crown each one of us personally; and may brotherly love and kindness dwell among us collectively. Amen.

W. BERLY, *President.*

The Constitutional term of the present officers having now expired, Synod proceeded to an election for officers, which resulted in the choice of the following:

OFFICERS OF SYNOD.

Rev. T. S. BOINEST, *President.*
Rev. PAUL DERRICK, *Recording Secretary.*
Rev. Prof. J. P. SMELTZER, *Corresponding Secretary.*
Maj. P. E. WISE, *Treasurer of Synod.*
Mr. J. F. SCHIRMER, *Treasurer of Seminary.*
Maj. J. P. KINARD, *Treasurer of Widow's Fund.*

Letters, documents, etc., having reference to Synod, were called for and handed in for reference to the appropriate committees.

Synod now adjourned until to-morrow morning, 9½ o'clock.

Prayer by Rev. Dr. Bachman.

SECOND SESSION.

FRIDAY MORNING, October 13.

Synod met at 9½ o'clock and was opened with singing and prayer, by Rev. S. Bouknight.

The roll was called, and the brethren answered to their names.

The minutes of yesterday were read and confirmed.

The President announced that Rev. J. H. Cupp had been elected by the Ministerium, a member of this Synod.

Rev. B. Kreps, and J. D. Sease, Esq., of Rev. B. F. Berry's charge, appeared and took their seats.

The President announced the following standing committees:

1. *On Unfinished Business*—Rev. A. W. Lindler and J. S. Derrick.

2. *On President's Report*—Revs. Prof. Smeltzer, Bolles and Mr. J. J. Rauch.

3. *On Letters and Petitions*—Revs. Berly, Dufford, and Mr. S. P. Dickert.

4. *On State of Religion*—Revs. Cupp, Bouknight and Wertz.

5. *On Synodical Fund*—Messrs. Chisolm and Wise.

6. *On Widows' Fund*—Messrs. Keller and Rikard.

Rev. Prof. Smeltzer, Corresponding Secretary, not having received or written letters, had nothing to report.

Rev. Prof. Smeltzer stated that Maj. Summer, Secretary of the Trustees of Newberry College, had no report to make.

The Secretary of the Board of Seminary, stated that he had not attended to any business and hence he had nothing to report.

Parochial reports were called for, in connection with them the pastors read their narrative on the State of Religion.

PAROCHIAL REPORT.

NAMES OF PASTORS.	Congregations.	Infants Baptized. White.	Infants Baptized. Colored.	Members Received by Baptism. White.	Members Received by Baptism. Colored.	Members Received by Confirmat'n. White.	Members Received by Confirmat'n. Colored.	Members Received by Certificate. White.	Members Received by Certificate. Colored.	Dismissions. White.	Dismissions. Colored.	Communicants. White.	Communicants. Colored.	Death of Members. Adults.	Death of Members. Infants.	Prayer Meetings.	Sabbath Schools. Schools.	Sabbath Schools. Teachers.	Sabbath Schools. Scholars.	Contributions. Synod.	Contributions. Missionary Society.	Contributions. Other Societies.	Contributions. Local Objects.	Benevolent Societies.
Rev. Dr. Bachman....	1	46	31	3		48		14			75	*	20	13			1			$16 00				2
Rev. T. S. Boinest....	3	10		5		57		4				420	23	10	2	1	1	5	25	30 00				1
Rev. S. Bouknight....	2	4		2	1	4		4		1		271	101	6	1	2	2	14	65	10 68				1
Rev. B. F. Berry. ...	1					5						84		2		1								1
Rev. J. H. Cupp......	1	2		2					1			61		4						8 00				2
Rev. W. Berly.......	2	2										182	2	1	2									
Rev. Paul Derrick....	2	4	5			1					10	122	100	7			2	8	40	32 68	$12 00			1
Rev. J. N. Derrick....	1	3				2		1				38												
Rev. B. Kreps........	1	1		6		10		2		2		139	15	3	1	1	1	4	24	2 00				
Rev. A. W. Lindler...	2	2	6									110	5	2						6 95				
Rev. J. P. Smeltzer...	1			1								50					1	8	25	8 90				
Rev. J. H. W. Wertz.	3	3		3		14						164	10	3		1	2	8	50					
Rev. A. D. L. Moser..	1	4	1			11						54		1		1	1	2	18	4 00				
Rev. J. A. Sligh......	1	3	17			1	28	1		1		12	98	1			1	4	40	5 90				
Rev. J. Hawkins......	3	3		4		13						160					1	7	35					
Rev. E. Caughman....	2	5		3		16						116		4		1	1	6	30					
Rev. W. S. Bowman..	1	6	4	2	1	6	2	3			18	64	11	2	2	1	1	11	65	10 00	15 00		$100 00	
Rev. W. A. Houck...	2	5	3	3	3	10	5					150	*	2	3		2	6	20	11 50				
Total...............	30	103	67	34	5	198	55	29	1	4	103	2197	385	61	11	9	17	83	463	$145 71	$27 00		$100 00	8

☞ A number of Pastors made no report.

*The number doubtful.

Synodical Collections were called for, and were thus registered:

SYNODICAL CONTRIBUTIONS.

Rev. Dr. Bachman's charge—		
St. John's, Charleston,		$16 00
Rev. B. Kreps' charge—		
Mt. Calvary,		2 00
Rev. A. D. L. Moser's charge—		
Mt. Zion,		4 00
Rev. T. S. Boinest's charge—		
Bethlehem,	11 00	
St. John's,	10 30	
St. Luke's,	8 60—	30 00
Rev. W. A. Houck's charge—		
Trinity,	8 50	
Pine Grove,	3 00—	11 50
Rev. J. H. W. Wertz's charge—		
Corinth,	2 00	
Union,	2 00	
Salem,	2 00—	6 00
Rev. A. W. Lindler's charge—		
Trinity,	3 25	
St. John's,	2 45	
Mt. Zion,	1 25—	6 95
Rev. E. Bouknight's charge—		
St. Mark's,	6 68	
Macedonia,	4 00—	10 68
Rev. W. Berly's charge—		
St. Stephen's		1 30
Rev. Prof. Smeltzer's charge—		
Luther Chapel,		8 90
Rev. J. H. Cupp's charge—		
Sandy Run,		8 00
Rev. Paul Derrick's charge—		
St. Mathews' and Mt. Lebanon,		32 68
Rev. D. M. Blackwelder's charge—		
St. Paul's,		5 33
Rev. W. S. Bowman's charge—		
Morris Street Church, Charleston,		10 00
Rev. . A. Sligh's charge—		
Newville,		5 00
Total.		$158 39

The hour for preaching having arrived, Synod adjourned by rising.

At 11 o'clock, Rev. J. H. Cupp preached from Heb. III. 12.

Upon resuming business, Synod proceeded to an election to fill the vacancies occurring in the Board of Directors of Seminary, which resulted in the re-election of the former members:

CLASSIFICATION OF BOARD OF DIRECTORS.

Class of 1863.	*Class of* 1864.	*Class of* 1865.
Rev. A. R. Rude.	Rev. D. M. Blackwelder.	Dr. Bachman.
Rev. T. S. Boinest.	Rev. W. S. Bowman.	Rev. S. Bouknight.
Mr. H. Gallman.	Capt. J. P. Aull.	Mr. J. F. Schirmer.
Mr. W. W. Houseal.	Capt. W. K. Bachman.	Dr. G. Muller.

Rev. T. S. Boinest was re-elected Corresponding Delegate to Synod of North Carolina, and Rev. D. M. Blackwelder his alternate.

To the Synod of Georgia, Rev. W. S. Bowman was re-elected, and Rev. Prof. Smeltzer his alternate.

Pending the election of delegates to the General Synod, Rev. Berly offered the following resolution which was adopted:

Resolved, That the alternates to the General Synod, whose names stand recorded opposite the primaries, be the alternates of such primaries.

The election of delegates to General Synod, resulted in the re-election of the former delegates, excepting H. C. Franck, deceased, whose place was filled by the election of J. M. Witt. The names of delegates to General Synod stand thus:

Principals.	*Alternates.*
Rev. W. Berly.	Rev. T. S. Boinest.
" N. Aldrich.	" E. A. Bolles.
" C. F. Bansemer.	" S. Bouknight.
" D. M. Blackwelder.	" E. Caughman.
Prof. Smeltzer.	" Paul Derrick.
Dr. G. Muller.	Maj. P. E. Wise.
Mr. J. W. Dreher.	Mr. J. M. Witt.
Mr. F. A. Brahe.	Mr. R. H. Zimmerman.
Maj. J. P. Kinard.	Mr. J. Barre.
Mr. W. W. Houseal.	Mr. J. H. Graman.

Dr. Bachman offered the following preambles and resolutions, which were received:

WHEREAS, We have been informed, that a considerable number of farmers and mechanics from several portions of Germany, have expressed a willingness to emigrate to our Southern country, and become citizens, and as the great majority of them adhere to the faith of our Church, it is our duty to make such provisions for their religious instruction as will preserve them the advantages and comforts of religion.

WHEREAS, The exigencies of our country require, that changes should be made in our industrial pursuits, and that the time has arrived when emigrants from abroad should be encouraged to settle among us: Therefore,

Resolved, That a Committee of five be appointed from this body, to consider the propriety of devising some plan of introducing into our country a number of German emigrants, for the purpose of cultivating our soil, and of performing the duties of planters, farmers, graziers, horticulturists, mechanics and gardeners.

Resolved, That said Committee report to this body at its present session.

Committee, Dr. Bachman, Rev. Prof. Smeltzer, R. G. Chisolm, R. H. Zimmerman and Hon. J. Townsend.

Synod now adjourned until 9½ o'clock, a. m., to-morrow.

Prayer by Rev. J. D. W. Crook.

THIRD SESSION.

SATURDAY MORNING, October 14.

Synod met at the appointed time, and was opened with prayer by Rev. B. Kreps.

The roll was called, and the minutes of yesterday were read, corrected and confirmed.

The Secretary being unwell, Rev. J. H. Cupp was requested to act as his assistant.

The Committee on Seminary Fund made the following report, which was adopted:

The Committee to whom was referred the account of the Treasurer of the Theological Seminary, of the Lutheran Synod of South Carolina and adjacent States beg leave, respectfully, to report, that said account simply makes an exhibit of a balance in Confederate money of $45.75. Not a single entry of receipt or expenditure.

The list of assets, however, show an amount of near $30,000, but, of this, your Committee regret to say one-half will in all probability be a total loss. And even of those securities, which may be eventually paid, a small part, if any of the interest accruing on same, can be collected for some time, owing to the impoverished condition of our people and those institutions, and corporations, whose bonds and stocks constitute the Seminary Fund. Respectfully submitted,

R. G. CHISOLM.
P. E. WISE.

Rev. W. S. Bowman appeared and took his seat.

Rev. W. Berly read the report of the Committee on Letters and Petitions, which was received, considered by items, and adopted as a whole.

Item 4th in said report was received only as information.

REPORT OF THE COMMITTEE ON LETTERS.

The Committee appointed to report on Letters submit the following:

No. 1, Is a letter from W. W. Houseal, Esq., Treasurer of Synod, stating that he would not be able to attend Synod, as he would be under the necessity of attending the Court of Common Pleas for Newberry, as Sheriff of that District. He further states, that he could not send up his report as Treasurer, because some funds had been contributed after the adjournment of Synod at its last meeting; the exact amount of which he did not recollect, and had not time to get a statement from the Secretary. He requests this body also to relieve him from serving any longer as its Treasurer.

No. 2, Is a letter from the Rev. E. Caughman, in which he gives as his reason for absence from this meeting, his age, the distance, and the condition of the country. As brother Caughman has been present with us on all former occasions, we recommend that he be excused. He sends one dollar as a contribution to the Missionary Fund, which we herewith present.

No. 3, Is a letter from the Rev. Jacob Moser, informing us that age and infirmity prevent him from participating in our ecclesiastical deliberations. He asks this body to excuse his non-attendance at our present meeting, and assures us that he will ever pray for the prosperity of our beloved Zion. We cheerfully recommend that brother Moser be excused.

No. 4, Is a letter from Mrs. F. C. Ring, applying to this Synod for pecuniary aid.

No. 5, Is a letter from Mr. Jacob F. Schirmer, Treasurer of the Seminary Fund, sending up his report, and informing this body that circumstances beyond his control would prevent him from being present with us. He requests to be excused; and your Committee recommend that his request be granted.

Respectfully submitted,

W. BERLY, *Chairman.*
E. DUFFORD.
SIMON P. DICKERT.

Mr. R. G. Chisolm offered the following resolution:

Resolved, That a Committee be appointed to examine the account of Treasurer of Synod, so that said account may be embodied in the minutes, before the printing of the same.

Committee, Dr. O. B. Mayer and Capt. W. G. Metts.

The following brethren were excused, by verbal statements, from non-attendance at the present meeting of Synod: Revs. D. M. Blackwelder, W. Eichelberger, J. M. Schreckhise, B. F. Berry, D. Sheely and M. Rauch.

The Committee on the President's Report, offered the following which was adopted:

Your Committee would report that as the only subject presented in the President's report, for the action of this body, is the present condition and future prospects of Newberry College, your Committee would offer the following:

Resolved, That the Corresponding Secretary inform the Board of Trustees, that it is the desire of Synod that its members should meet the first Wednesday of November, to open again the College and appoint Professors.

Respectfully submitted,

J. P. SMELTZER.
E. A. BOLLES.
J. I. RAUCH.

Mr. R. G. Chisolm asked and obtained leave of absence after Sunday.

Synod adjourned to meet at the call of the President, in order to allow the Missionary Society to hold its annual meeting.

Prayer by Rev. W. S. Bowman.

At two o'clock Synod resumed business.

Hon. J. Townsend was invited to a seat as an advisory member of Synod.

The following resolution was offered by Rev. W. Berly:

Resolved, That article 13, chapter i. of the Constitution of Synod be so amended, as to read as follows: Any number of ministers, or ministers and lay-delegates assembled at the designated time and place, for the regular annual or extra meeting of Synod, shall constitute a quorum for the transaction of business.

The resolution, according to the Constitution, was laid upon the table for action, at the next meeting of Synod.

Mr. R. G. Chisolm read the report of the Committee on German Immigration, which was considered by items, and finally adopted as a whole.

The Committee, to whom was referred the subject of German Immigration, have had a meeting, and beg leave respectfully to present the following Preamble and Resolutions, as conveying the views of said Committee:

I. WHEREAS, since the freeing of the slaves, the only labor by which our Southern soil was cultivated and made to yield such rich and abundant harvest, our Southern country has been deprived, to a considerable extent, of the means wherewith, we, as a people, shall be supported.

II. AND WHEREAS, it has become now absolutely necessary that a large introduction into our country of laborers from over-crowded Europe, shall come among us, that our land may again yield of its abundance.

III. AND WHEREAS, this immigration may be sought for in protestant Germany, as being the people best adapted for the cultivating of the soil, &c.

IV. AND WHEREAS, that people are mainly of the persuasion and faith of the Lutheran Church. Therefore be it

Resolved, 1st. That we make every effort to encourage this immigration into our Southern States, and moreover that this immigration be from protestant Germany.

Resolved, 2nd. That a Committee of Correspondence be appointed, whose chairman shall take immediate steps to lay this matter before Pastors of Lutheran Churches in Protestant Germany, stating the deep interest exhibited by this body, and the great anxiety our people have expressed to secure immigrants, as co-laborers with them in cultivating the soil, and various other pursuits.

Resolved, 3rd. That the Chairman, also, assure them, that every means shall be adopted by us to secure to them all the religious and educational privileges that we enjoy.

Resolved, 4th. That inasmuch as such immigrants would for a short time, at least, be unable to comprehend the English language; and therefore, could not enjoy the services of our Church to their spiritual improvement, that said Chairman recommend, that a Pastor should accompany each colony. Restpectfully submitted,

JOHN BACHMAN.
J. P. SMELTZER.
JOHN F. TOWNSEND.
R. H. ZIMMERMAN.
R. G. CHISOLM.

According to resolution second of said report, a committee of five, was appointed by the President, consisting of Dr. Bachman, Revs. L. Muller, A. R. Rude, Hon. J. Townsend, G. T. Berg, J. A. Wagener and W. Uferhardt.

Synod now adjourned till Monday morning, 9½ o'clock.

Prayer by Rev. Prof. Smeltzer.

SABBATH EXERCISES.

At 9½ o'clock a. m., a large congregation having collected, religious services were conducted by Rev. A. W. Lindler.

Rev. T. S. Boinest, at 10½ o'clock, addressed a large and attentive audience from 2 Cor. 16, 13.

Dr. Bachman followed with a suitable address, preparatory to the communion, and consecrated the elements emblematical of our Lord's death; after which a large number of the followers of Christ united in commemorating his dying love.

After an intermission of half an hour, the congregation re-assembled, and Rev. Prof. J. P. Smeltzer, delivered a very interesting sermon, from Deut. 11, 31.

Revs. J. H. W. Wertz and A. D. L. Moser, held religious services Saturday and Sunday nights, at Mrs. Mary and G. Gates.

Thus ended the exercises of the Holy Sabbath to the edification and strengthening of many of the followers of the Redeemer.

FOURTH SESSION.

Monday Morning, October 16.

Synod met at 9½ o'clock, and was opened with prayer by Rev. W. A. Houck.

The roll was called and the Minutes of Saturday were read and confirmed.

Rev. J. H. Cupp read the report of the Committee on the State of Religion, which was received and adopted.

REPORT OF COMMITTEE ON THE STATE OF RELIGION.

The reports on the State of Religion in the different charges belonging to this Synod, which have been referred to us for examination, furnish us with a striking exemplification of the glorious fact, verified in the gracious experience of our common Christianity, that vital godliness is not a plant that finds a congenial soil only in the sunshine of prosperity—flourishing most, and producing its fruit only in an atmosphere and climate where there is an abundance of everything else to satisfy the wants of man. But the history of our Churches, during the brief period embraced by these reports, as well as the history of the Church from the beginning, demonstrates that the grace of God is a tree of life, taking root in, and fertilizing the most barren soil—flourishing rather more in the darkness of adversity than in the sunshine of prosperity—producing the only fruit that will satisfy the hunger of the soul in every condition of life—and bearing the only leaves that "are for the healing of the nations." In the disastrous war, through which we have just passed, both Church and State, have been submitted to the most fiery ordeal, that the people of this continent have ever experienced. The staring eyes of all other nations have been fixed upon the progress of transpiring events, to see "what the end of these things would be"—what would be the moral and religious effects of the revolutionary process which this country was undergoing. What have been, and what will be the political results of the trying crucible through which God has just taken us—whether for the elevation or degradation of this Southern land in the scale of political existence, it is not the province of this report, even to express an opinion. We are here for the investigation of matters pertaining to the Kingdom of Heaven, and not to legislate on questions of political economy. We are here not to inquire whether it is lawful to give tribute to Cæsar or not, but whether we have rendered unto God the things which were God's.

It has truly been said, "that war is demoralizing, has become a matter of history." The political convulsions with which our country has been afflicted, have materially affected the welfare of our Churches. Some of our sanctuaries have been committed to the flames by the barbarous hands of our vandalic invaders, and our people driven to places uncomfortable and inconvenient to worship their God. The destruction of a vast amount of property, which the laws of civilized warfare would have protected, has greatly crippled the benevolent enterprises and operations of the Church, and retarded her prosperity. Thousands of our young men, on whom the hopes of the Church, to a very great extent depended, for future success, have nobly fallen in defence of their country. Thousands of others have come to their death by diseases contracted from exposure to the hardships of the camp. And still thousands more, have died far away from the tender care and kind sympathies of home, in cold and inhospitable prisons. Many affectionate hearts have been broken, and many homes been sadly bereaved by the loss of fathers, husbands, brothers and friends. Many have returned to their homes so corrupted in their morals, that they will be, at least for the present, lost to the Church. But whilst this has been the case in many instances, the friends of religion have been agreeably disappointed to see the great majority of our young men, who were permitted to return in safety to their homes, as free from immorality as when they left. And, many who had no concern about the salvation of their souls when they left, have come back with their hearts full of love to God. Numbers of young men, who had their portion in this world, when they returned and found their homes and property destroyed, and the idols of their hearts removed, determined to give themselves to the service of God, and lay up for themselves "treasures in Heaven."

The fiery trials through which, in the Providence of God, we have been called to pass, have also had a purifying effect upon the Church. Many nominal professors, who loved the world more than they loved God, but who had no test to develope to the world their true characters, have yielded to the temptations of "filthy lucre," extortion and speculation, and like chaff, have been sifted out. Some who, like a certain wicked sailor, when they were sailing upon a smooth sea, thought themselves safe, and neglected the duty of prayer, when the storm of adversity came, found themselves unprepared to meet it, became alarmed and convicted, and were led by repentance to the mercy seat of Christ, and obtained the pardon of their sins. Others who really had the love of God in their hearts, the light of whose grace was swallowed up in the sunshine of prosperity, when the dark night of adversity came, their christian graces were made to appear as stars of considerable magnitude, and shined for the good of the world, and the honor and glory of God.

The Lord has also visited some of our Churches with precious seasons of revival, which have resulted in the addition of many souls of such, as we trust, will ultimately be saved. We have reason to believe that a better day for the Church is not far distant, when the watchmen of Zion will be able to report more glorious things concerning the City of our God. One sad feature, however, in the history of our Churches during the past year, we have yet to mention. Our colored members who were generally faithful in attending the preaching of the word and the ordinances of the Church, have forsaken both, and become vagrant, idle and demoralized to a fearful extent. Whether their new friends have advised them to seek a different road to Heaven, from that of their former guardians, we cannot tell. We sincerely hope that something better for the spiritual welfare of this unfortunate people may soon transpire.

Respectfully submitted,

J. H. CUPP.
S. BOUKNIGHT.
J. H. W. WERTZ.

The Committee on Widow's Fund, made the following report. Adopted.

The Committee to whom was referred the account of Treasurer of Widow's Fund, beg leave to report: That they have received no papers from the hand of the Treasurer, and therefore, are unable to make any report. Respectfully submitted,

J. D. KELLER.
H. W. RIKARD.

In relation to this report, Prof. Smeltzer remarked, that Maj. Kinard requested him to state to Synod, that he had collected some of the notes due the Widow's Fund, and there still remained in his hands one available note.

The following resolution was offered by Rev. W. Berly:

Resolved, That the Secretary have five hundred copies of the Minutes of last and of the present meeting printed. Adopted.

Rev. W. Berly offered the following resolution, which was adopted:

Resolved, That a Committee be appointed to examine the Archives of Synod, and ascertain how far back the Minutes of Synod have not been regularly recorded, and report to this body at its next meeting.

Committee—Revs. Prof. Smeltzer, J. Hawkins and J. A. Sligh.

Rev. A. W. Lindler offered the following, which was adopted:

Resolved, That the thanks of this Synod are due to the congregation of St. Matthew's Church, Orangeburg District. and to the citizens of the vicinity, for the kind hospitality received at their hands during our present meeting, and that they be tendered immediately after divine services by the President.

Synod now adjourned for divine services.

At 11 o'clock, Rev. S. Bouknight preached from Psalm 50, 14.

After a short recess, Synod resumed business.

Dr. Bachman moved that the same Board of Trustees of Newberry College be re-elected, which was concurred in.

St. Mark's Church, Edgefield District, S. C., was chosen as the next place of the meeting of Synod, and the following resolution offered by Rev. W. Berly:

Resolved, That this Synod meet on Thursday before the third

Sunday in October next, and that we meet annually on that day, until otherwise ordered. Adopted.

Rev. A. W. Lindler read the report of the Committee on Unfinished Business. Adopted.

The Committee on Unfinished Business, respectfully report, that they have carefully examined the Minutes, and find but one item worthy the notice of this body. On page nine of the manuscript Minutes, is a resolution, requiring the delegate to the North Carolina Synod to make inquiry as to a resolution passed by that body, concerning some money which was ordered to be paid over to our Seminary fund. Your Committee recommend, that inasmuch as the delegate has been unable to make the inquiry the Synod required, Therefore

Resolved, That he be requested to make the inquiry at the next meeting of the North Carolina Synod. Respectfully submitted,

A. W. LINDLER.
J. S. DERRICK.

There being a deficiency in the funds of Synod to defray the expenses of having the Minutes of last year and of the present meeting printed, Capt. H. W. Rikard proposed to be one of thirty to raise an additional one hundred and fifty dollars. The proposition was sustained, and the following resolution offered:

Resolved, That the names of the donors who have so generously come forward and contributed to defray the expenses of printing our proceedings, be inserted in the Minutes, with the amount contributed thereto appended:

NAMES OF CONTRIBUTORS.

Dr. J. A. Keller	$10 00	Miss Nancy Felkel	$1 00
Capt. H. W. Rikard	5 00	Miss Carrie Mitchell	1 00
Dr. Bachman	5 00	M. A. E. Haigler	1 00
Rev. Prof. Smeltzer	5 00	Capt. J. N. Haigler	1 00
Maj. P. E. Wise	5 00	Mr. James A. Dantzler	1 00
Rev. J. N. Derrick	5 00	Mrs. A. C. Dantzler	1 00
Rev. W. S. Bowman	5 00	Mrs. A. G. Gates	2 00
Mr. J. I. Rauch	5 00	Mrs. A. S. Riser	2 50
Rev. S. Bouknight	5 00	Mr. N. I. Gates	2 00
Mr. S. P. Dickert	5 00	Mr. N. Stroman	1 00
Rev. T. S. Boinest	5 00	Rev. W. A. Houck	5 00
Capt. J. W. Sellers	5 00	Mrs. Mary Gates	2 00
Mr. H. Zimmerman	5 00	Mrs. Louisa Gates	2 00
Rev. A. W. Lindler	5 00	Mrs. M. B. Haigler	1 00
Mrs. R. H. Zimmerman	2 00	Miss Agnes C. Haigler	1 00
Rev. J. A. Sligh	5 00	Mrs. Sarah Bull	2 50
Miss H. C. Barber	2 50	H. L. Rickenbacher	1 00

Miss Alice Barber............	2 50	H. Cobia, Esq................	5 00
Dr. J. E. Holman............	2 00	Mrs. J. W. Sellers............	5 00
Mr. J. W. Barber............	2 50	William Keller..............	5 00
Mr. B. W. Keller............	2 50	H. A. Haigler...............	5 00
Miss Jane Wissenhurst........	1 00	R. G. Chisolm, Esq...........	5 00
J. D. Keller................	5 00		
Total			$153 00

Rev. W. S. Bowman submitted the following resolution, which was adopted:

Resolved, That the thanks of this body be tendered to the agents and proprietors of the "Charleston Daily News," and "Charleston Daily Courier," for their *gratuitous* publication of a notice of our present Convention.

The following resolution was offered by Rev. W. S. Bowman, which was adopted:

Resolved, That if there be a deficiency in the collections of Synod to have the Minutes, both of last year, and of the present meeting printed, that the Secretary be authorized to have the proceedings only of the present meeting printed.

Resolved, That the Missionary Society be allowed to publish their Minutes in connection with ours. Adopted.

Synod ordered that Mrs. Ring, Cloy and Leppard, each receive $50,00 from the Widow's Fund, provided that amount be in the Treasury, if not, whatever amount remains, to be equally divided between them.

Synod now adjourned to meet at the time and place above specified.

Prayer by Rev. Dr. Bachman.

PAUL DERRICK,
Recording Sec'y. of Synod of So. Ca., and adjacent States.

Wm. W. Houseal, *in account with the Evangelical Lutheran Synod of South Carolina.*

DR.

	Cash on hand at meeting of Synod Oct. 1864,	$285 00
1864 Oct 16	Received as contributions from Churches at Synod, held at Beth Eden Church,	1587 50
" "	Received interest on Rev. J. H. B.'s note,	100 00
1865 Jan 16	Received interest and principal on Rev. D. J. Dreher's note,	282 96
		$2255 46

CR.

1863 Nov 1	Paid Rev. T. S. Boinest,	$ 24 81
1864 Oct 23	Paid Rev. T. S. Boinest's expenses as delegate to Georgia Synod,	50 00
1865 Aug 30	Paid Evans & Cogswell for printing Minutes of Synod,	1360 00
	Balance cash on hand,	820 65
		$2255 46

SUPPLEMENTARY STATEMENT.

Amount notes on hand,	$1122 76
Interest bearing Treasury notes,	1000 00
4 per cent Certificate,	700 00
Cash (Confederate Treasury notes,)	820 65
	$3643 41

We, the Committee, appointed by Synod to examine Treasurer's account, find upon examination, that he has faithfully and correctly discharged his duty.

O. B. MAYER,
G. W. METZ, } Committee.

Minutes of the Ministerium.

FIRST SESSION.

THURSDAY, October 12, 1865.

The Ministerium met at 2 o'clock, p. m., and was opened with prayer by Rev. E. Dufford,

Rev. W. Berly presented the honorable dismission of Rev. J. H. Cupp of the Synod of Virginia; and on motion he was unanimously received into connection with this Ministerium.

Rev. W. Berly read a letter from Rev. J. Hawkins, stating that he had taken charge of Churches within the bounds of this Ministerium, and wished connection with it, whereupon, it was

Resolved, That he be received by furnishing his dismission from the Synod of Georgia.

The Sermons and Journals of licentiates were called for, and referred to the following Committees:

Rev. J. A. Sligh's to Revs. Cupp and Bouknight.

Rev. A. D. L. Moser's to Revs. Houck and Lindler.

The Ministerium adjourned to meet at the call of the President.

Prayer by Rev. J. H. W. Wertz.

SECOND SESSION.

SATURDAY EVENING, October 14.

The Ministerium met, and was opened with prayer by Rev. J. N. Derrick. The Minutes of the last Session were read and confirmed.

Rev. W. Berly offered the following:

WHEREAS, the Rev. A. Angerer of Walhalla, Pickens Dist., S. C., applied to and received from the former President of this Ecclesiastical body, a letter of dismission from this Synod, to connect himself with the Evangelical Lutheran Synod of Maryland; and whereas, facts have been disclosed to this Ministerium at its present meeting, affecting the moral character of the said Angerer. Therefore

Resolved, That the Corresponding Secretary, address a letter to the President of the Evangelical Lutheran Synod of Maryland, informing him, that the former President had no knowledge of the facts now disclosed, when he favored the said Angerer with a certificate of dismission from this body. Adopted.

Rev. J. H. Cupp presented the report of the Committee on the Sermon and Journal of Rev. J. A. Sligh, which was accepted and adopted.

The documents placed in our hands for examination, are the sermon and journal of Rev. J. A. Sligh.

The sermon has for its subject the 14th verse of the 6th chapter of Gal,, and does honor to both the head and heart of its author. The arrangement is appropriate and natural. It is well conceived, well written, and sound in doctrine.

The journal shows that Brother Sligh has been actively and usefully engaged in the Master's work—having preached during the past Synodical year forty sermons, assisted in the administration of the Lord's supper nine times, baptised twenty persons, admitted to membership twenty-eight by confirmation and baptism, attended three funerals, and performed other ministerial acts—all giving credence that he has the qualifications of both preacher and pastor. Your Committee recommend his license be continued.

Respectfully submitted,

J. H. CUPP.
SAMUEL BOUKNIGHT.

Rev. W. A. Houck read the report of the Committee on the Sermon and Journal of Rev. A. D. L. Moser. Received and adopted.

The Committee to whom were referred the sermon and journal of Rev. A. D. L. Moser, beg leave to report:

That the journal exhibits a commendable degree of industry and faithfulness on the part of the brother, and the sermon is creditable alike to the piety and attainments of the author.

Your Committee, with pleasure, recommend that this brother's license be renewed.

Respectfully submitted,

W. A. HOUCK.
A. W. LINDLER.

Rev. W. Berly offered the following resolution, which was received and adopted :

Resolved, That brother S. P. Dickert be received as a student of Theology, under the direction of this Synod, and that he be placed under the direction and instruction of Rev. T. S. Boinest, and he be required to attend the annual meetings of this Ministerium, and submit to a regular examination.

The Ministerium having now completed its business, adjourned with prayer by Rev. W. A. Houck.

PAUL DERRICK,

Recording Secretary of the Evangelical Lutheran Ministerium of South Carolina and adjacent States.

Minutes of Missionary Society.

SATURDAY, October 14, 1865.

At 11 o'clock, according to previous appointment, Rev. A. D. L. Moser delivered the annual Missionary Sermon, from Matt. 9, 37, 38.

The President being absent, the first Vice President, Rev. Dr. Bachman, took the chair.

After a brief and impressive statement of the circumstances under which the Society met, by the acting Vice President, a Committee was appointed to wait upon the congregation to solicit contributions for the constitution of members to the Society, which resulted in the following list of membership:

INDIVIDUAL CONTRIBUTIONS.

Name	Amount	Name	Amount
Rev. J. P. Smeltzer	$1 00	Rev. W. A. Houck	1 00
Mrs. A. E. Smeltzer	1 00	Capt. H. W. Rikard	1 00
Mrs. Sarah Smeltzer	1 00	Rev. J. H. W. Wertz	1 00
Master S. S. Smeltzer	1 00	Capt. J. N. Haigler	1 00
Miss H. E. Smeltzer	1 00	Rev. B. Kreps	1 00
Charlie M. Smeltzer	1 00	D. J. Zeigler	1 00
J. Bachman Smeltzer	1 00	Maj. P. E. Wise	1 00
S. Kate Smeltzer	1 00	J. I. Rauch	1 00
Rev. W. Berly	1 00	W. E. Barber	1 00
Rev. J. Bachman, D. D	1 00	J. S. Derrick	1 00
Rev. J. A. Sligh	1 00	Rev. A. W. Lindler	1 00
Mrs. A. R. Sligh	1 00	Rev. A. D. L. Moser	2 50
Rev. T. S. Boinest	2 50	Capt. W. G. Metts	1 00
Mrs. T. S. Boinest	2 50	S. P. Dickert	1 00
Rev. E. Caughman	1 00	R. G. Chisolm	1 00
Rev. W. S. Bowman	1 00	Mrs. R. G. Chisolm	1 00
Rev. S. Bouknight	1 00	Rev. J. D. W. Crook	1 00
Mrs. A. G. Gates	1 00	Mrs. Mary Gates	1 00
Mrs. E. R. Zimmerman	2 00	Mrs. J. A. Keller	1 00
Mrs. W. A. Houck	1 00	Miss M. D. Haigler	1 00
Mrs. M. B. Haigler	1 00	Mrs. Sarah Bull	1 00
W. R. Keller	1 00	Mrs. J. W. Barber	1 00
M. J. Keller	1 00	W. Keller	1 00
J. M. Shirer	1 00	James A. Dantzler	1 00
Hon. J. Townsend	1 00	W. F. Barton	1 09
Dr. J. C. Holman	1 00	E. W. S. Gates	1 00
H. L. Richenbacher	1 00	F. J. Gates	1 00
J. M. Brendenburgh	1 00	F. P. Branbenburgh	1 00

Mrs. M. C. Barber	1 00	R. H. Zimmerman	1 00
Mrs. B. E. Jackson	1 00	Miss Anna Zimmerman	1 00
Mrs. Adrianna Sellers	1 00	Miss C. E. Fersner	1 00
Miss A. C. Zeigler	1 00	Miss J. E. Fersner	1 00
Miss H. C. Barber	1 00	E. H. Irick	1 00
J. L. Rast	1 00	J. D. Keller	1 00
J. H. Arant	1 00		
Total annual contributions,			$74 50

CONGREGATIONAL CONTRIBUTIONS.

Rev. Paul Derrick's charge, St. Matthews and Lebanon,	$12 00
Rev. W. S. Bowman's charge, Morris St. Luth. church,	15 00
Total congregation contributions,	$27 00

RECAPITULATION.

Annual contributions, - - - - - -	$74 50
Congregational contributions, - - - - -	27 00
	$101 50

The election for officers of the Society, resulted in the re-election of all the former officers, with the exception of Rev. T. S. Boinest, whose place as Recording Secretary, was supplied by the election of Rev. Paul Derrick.

OFFICERS OF THE MISSIONARY SOCIETY.

Mr. J. F. Schirmer, *President.*

Revs. J. Bachman, D. D., W. S. Bowman and Maj. John P. Kinard, *Vice Presidents.*

Rev. Paul Derrick, *Recording Secretary.*

Rev. D. M. Blackwelder, *Corresponding Secretary.*

Mr. J. J. Dreher, *Treasurer.*

Revs. J. P. Smeltzer, J. M. Schreckhise, T. S. Boinest, Messrs. W. W. Houseal, M. Barre, John P. Kinard and J. J. Dreher, *Executive Committee.*

There was no report from the Corresponding Secretary.

The Treasurer's report was handed in and referred to a Committee.

Committee—Maj. P. E. Wise and Capt. H. W. Rikard.

It was moved, that Rev. W. S. Bowman be paid the amount

appropriated to him at the former meeting of the Society. So ordered.

The thanks of the Society were tendered Rev. A. D. L. Moser, for his interesting address.

Rev. J. A. Sligh was appointed to deliver the Missionary Sermon at our next annual meeting, and Rev. W. S. Bowman, his alternate.

Maj. P. E. Wise read the following, which was adopted:

The Committee to examine the Treasurer's account, report that they have discharged the duty, and find all correct, showing a balance in hands, in Confederate notes, amounting to $868,64.

Respectfully submitted,

P. E. WISE.
H. W. RIKARD.

Resolved, That we request the Synod to allow the Minutes of this Society to be published in connection with theirs.

The Society now adjourned to meet at 12 m., at the time and place of the next meeting of Synod.

PAUL DERRICK,
Recording Secretary of Missionary Society.

JOHN W. DREHER, *Assistant Treasurer, in account with Synodical Missionary Society of the Evangelical Lutheran Synod of South Carolina and adjacent States.*

1864	DR.	
Oct 17	Amount of notes in hand - - - - - - -	$ 16 14
	Amount on deposit in Saving's Bank - - -	201 36
	Amount of cash in hands from J. J. Dreher - -	901 14
		1118 64
		250 00
	Balance in hands in Confederate notes,	$868 64

1864	CR.	
Oct 17	To cash paid Rev. W. S. Bowman,	$250 00

J. W. DREHER, Assistant Treasurer.

October 8th, 1865.

www.ingramcontent.com/pod-product-compliance
Lightning Source LLC
Chambersburg PA
CBHW022152090426
42742CB00010B/1480
9783337844806